Redefining Business in the New Africa

Shifting Strategies to be Successful

Lauri E. Elliott
Hartmut Sieper
Nissi Ekpott

Published by Conceptualee, Inc.

Published by Conceptualee, Inc.:

301 McCollough Drive, 4th Floor
Charlotte, North Carolina 28262
United States

ISBN-13 9780983301516 Print Book
ISBN-13 9780983301547 Electronic Book
05042011

Chapter Contributors: Nwakego Eyisi, Jonathan Goldberg, and John Luiz
Book Cover Design by Vin Furlong
Front Cover Photo by Nissi Ekpott
Back Cover Photo by Hartmut Sieper
Foreword by Sipho Mseleku

Business & Economics / International / General

I pointed out to you the stars and all you saw was the tip of my finger.

(African Proverb)

Other titles and content on insights, resources, and strategy for business and investment in Africa can be explored at:

http://www.afribiz.info

http://www.afribiz.net

http://www.neuafrika.com

http://www.trans-africa-invest.com

Table of Contents

Preface
Nissi Ekpott

In 2007, I watched *Africa Open for Business*[1], a BBC award-winning documentary produced by Carol Pineau from Washington, DC. It showed ten African businesses from ten countries, randomly selected, hard at work, and succeeding against many odds. It contradicted most perceptions of Africa. I got a copy and traveled with it to the United States.

I showed it to friends in Iowa. The reactions were intense and varied. The Americans watched with interest and asked many questions. Some of the Africans burst into tears of joy - at last someone was showing Africa in a new light.

Two weeks later, I was traveling from Johannesburg to Cape Town in South Africa. I had been booked to fly economy, but at the boarding gate the airline benevolently upgraded me to business class. I took my seat, tucked myself in, and then turned to say "hi" to the lady beside me. It was Carol Pineau!

I knew that our meeting was no accident. We talked at length about the documentary and reasons behind it. The meeting made an impact on both of us. I got the sense that Carol saw a new future in Africa, and was working intently to show the world this future and also to be a part of it. I left knowing that things God had previously spoken to me about the African continent were unfolding.

Since then, the global focus on Africa has grown significantly. Some believe the *Africa Open for Business* documentary played a key role, but long before this there were many others who saw a renaissance coming in

---

[1] http://www.africaopenforbusiness.com

1

Africa, including Gunnar Olson, founder of the International Christian Chamber of Commerce and Thabo Mbeki, former president of South Africa.

Carol Pineau's documentary helped me shift from just having an expectation to applying practical, wisdom-filled steps in the area of business, which would allow us to harness these expected changes.

This book is designed to help readers achieve the shift from expectation to practical application. Our desire is to stir up, and see practically involved, people who are already convinced of Africa's restoration and renewal and its role in the future. For those who've had no inkling about the paradigm shifts on the continent and hear us, we encourage you to go and do your own research.

This book primarily targets business people. But, we believe everyone should read it.

We hope that, as you read through this book, you will share our belief in the continent and take practical steps to partake in the wealth, in all its facets, that this continent holds.

Also, we hope that you will be among those who shift from a focus only on aid to Africa, to a place of investing in viable business ventures, which is the only way to release wealth.

And, we hope that as you invest and contribute to change in Africa, you will find the power to change your lives for the better, sharing in the spiritual, physical, social, cultural, and economic wealth of Africa. Through our collective investment, Africa will be prepared to play its role as a place of refuge, abundant provision, healing, wisdom, and restoration to a dysfunctional, out-of-whack world.

Our sincere thanks to all those whose support has made this book a possibility. We are not able to mention all your names, but as you read this, you'll know who you are because you have invested directly, or indirectly, in the lives of the authors and producers of this book. True success is usually a collective effort. May God water your life abundantly.

Nissi Ekpott
January 11, 2011

Foreword

Sipho Mseleku

President, Pan African Chambers of Commerce and Industry

Redefining Business in the New Africa is one of the few excellently written and well-researched books on exploring business, trade, and investment opportunities on the African continent. It delves deeply into Africa's present, future, and the "kairos" moment for Africa to take its place as a leading citizen of the world, spiritually, socially, and economically.

As *Redefining Business* points out, Africa's vast economic, as well as trade and investment, opportunities remain mostly unexplored. The book also makes us see its pre-eminent place in the future political, as well as socioeconomic, global landscape.

Africa is a large continent, has vast natural, mineral, agricultural, forestry, water, and energy resources, and a growing consumer market. This presents great opportunities for business and economic development, which will result in Africa being able to exert political influence globally.

This book will be a powerful guide for global businesses intending to invest and expand into Africa. The book is also a powerful tool in the hands of African businesses to realize what has been bestowed in Africa and how they can tap into the opportunities presented by Africa for the betterment of all.

We, at the Global Business Roundtable, are privileged to be associated and working with the authors – Lauri, Hartmut, and Nissi.

Sipho Mseleku
President, Global Business Roundtable
President, Pan African Chambers of Commerce and Industry

About the Global Business Roundtable

The Global Business Roundtable is a platform and network for business people from various backgrounds and religions to come together to network and exchange ideas on business, career, and professional development. Its primary focus is on complete development of a person, including business development, skills development, wealth creation, estate planning, networking, mentorship, business and procurement opportunities, as well as spiritual development.

http://theglobalbusinessroundtable.ning.com/

Pan African Chambers of Commerce and Industry

The Pan African Chambers of Commerce and Industry (PACCI) is a continental chamber, representing 53 African countries. It is the single largest business body on the African continent. Its role is summed up in this phrase, "The voice of business in Africa".

The New Africa

1

Introduction:
The New Africa
Hartmut Sieper

While private wealth in developed nations struggles to recover from the economic crisis, the situation in Africa is remarkably bright. Africa, the colorful continent that consists of 53 nations (soon to be 54 nations with the secession of Southern Sudan from Northern Sudan) has prepared the stage for abundant wealth creation in this decade and beyond.

Major paradigm shifts can be observed in the world that will dramatically change current patterns and shape new global economic situations. First, Europe and the United States are experiencing great economic uncertainty, having started with financial uncertainty, now moving to economic problems, and later even to political insecurity and social unrest if not contained. Africa, on the other hand, will become more stable and will be considered less risky in the future. The view of Africa compared to the rest of the world will balance out.

Second, while media still lags behind in sharing positive headlines about Africa, there is a shift to more holistic reporting. The more success stories that are told about Africa, the more potential investors will pay attention to Africa as an investment destination that is worth considering.

Third, more African political and economic leaders are promoting foreign direct investments instead of development aid. They want to attract serious businesses and sincere investors to their countries. Companies and entrepreneurs are offered many investment incentives.

The classic concept of helping poor African nations by granting credit and donating goods and money is not the Africa of today. For example, Nigerian President Goodluck Jonathan stated, at the G8 African Leaders

Outreach at the G8/G20 Toronto Summit in June 2010, that his country would prefer removal of trade barriers over aid.

Development aid will successively be replaced by investments. In fact, the process is well underway. Foreign direct investment (FDI) to the continent reached $88 billion in 2008, according to the annual *African Economic Outlook*[2]. This was double the figure, provided by the Organization for Economic Co-operation and Development (OECD)[3], of $44 billion for net official development assistance (ODA) in 2008.

Fourth, today's Africa speaks for itself as a compelling investment case in six areas – macroeconomic stability and economic reform; low inclusion in world financial systems; fewer conflicts; abundant resources; a large, growing, under tapped consumer market; and a growing number of emerging versus developing economies.

---

[2] http://www.africaneconomicoutlook.org
[3] http://www.oecd.org

Macroeconomic Stability and Economic Reform

This is the Central Bank of West African States in Bamako, Mali. (Photo by: Hartmut Sieper)

The macroeconomic situation is favorable. Short-, medium-, and long-term growth can be expected for most countries. Growth in Sub-Saharan Africa in 2010 is estimated at 5%, according to the International Monetary Fund (IMF).[4] In 2011, growth is forecast to reach 5.5%. Compare this to a growth forecast under 3% in Western economies, according to the *Global Economic Prospects 2011*[5] by the World Bank. In fact, expectations for Sub-Saharan Africa's growth exceed those for global growth (3.3%) overall.

---

[4] http://www.imf.org
[5] World Bank. (January 2011). Global Economic Prospects 2011. Accessed online at http://web.worldbank.org/WBSITE/EXTERNAL/EXTDEC/ EXTDECPROSPECTS/GEPEXT/0,,contentMDK:22804791~pagePK:51087946~piP K:51087916~theSitePK:538110,00.html (January 20, 2011).

Also, governments have demonstrated strong commitment to economic reforms, which has resulted in improved legal frameworks for investors and companies. A good example is the introduction of one-stop shops that allow foreign investors to found companies in a few days, compared with the norm of several weeks or even months. In Rwanda, you only need three days to launch a company. To found a company in Botswana from Europe, one can do all the paperwork at the London office of the Botswana Export Development and Investment Agency (BEDIA).

Low Inclusion in the World's Financial Systems

Africa's low inclusion into the world's financial systems, which was considered negative in the past, is now revealed to be a blessing. Toxic assets have not found their way into balance sheets of most African banks. Asset price bubbles, fired by credit inflation, could not develop because of limited availability of loans and high interest rates. There is no excess liquidity in Africa that could have led to artificially high prices. Where asset prices are high, the main reason is a combination of elevated demand and lack of supply. Africa has shown an impressive robustness against the world financial and economic crisis.

Note: *Africa did experience varying levels of disruption in trade and investment due to the global economic crisis. However, these areas are on the rebound. As mentioned before, Sub-Saharan Africa is expected to experience broad-based growth in 2011 at about 5.5%.*

Fewer Conflicts

The decline in political conflicts and wars makes Africa less risky. While the news still often reports of the eastern Democratic Republic of Congo (DRC), Somalia, and Sudan, as well as recent upheavals in Cote d'Ivoire, Tunisia, Egypt, Algeria, and Libya, investors should remember that these are a few out of 53 countries.

There is a strong trend towards democratic or open forms of government. Also, stronger institutions are on the rise.

Natural Resources

This is a copper facility in Zambia. (Photo by: Hartmut Sieper)

Africa's natural resources are not only abundant but diverse. A number of countries have many natural resources. For example, the DRC has abundant water, arable land, and dozens of different mineral resources, including gold, copper, uranium, diamonds, and coltan.

Many regions are severely under explored. Increased exploration activities may lead to positive surprises and unexpected results like the offshore oil fields in Ghana, as well as newly discovered coal deposits in Mozambique and diamond fields in Zimbabwe.

Large Consumer Markets

The African population grew to 1 billion in 2010 and will reach over 2 billion in 2050 while Western populations will shrink. The five largest countries in 2010 by population were Nigeria (152 million), Ethiopia (88 million), Egypt (80 million), DRC (71 million), and South Africa (49 million), according to *The World Factbook*.

Vijay Mahajan, author of *Africa Rising: How 900 Million African Consumers Offer More Than You Think*[6], says there is a large middle class with unmet needs in Africa. This middle class needs basic services like housing, energy, education, health, food, and transport. They have money to pay for it. They are unlike their Western counterparts who carry too much debt.

However, the African middle class, like other middle classes in developing countries, does not have average annual incomes upward of $30,000 like the Western middle class. On the other hand, the large, potential market can offset this for businesses and investors.

These consumer markets are also fragmented. Many countries have fewer than 5 million people. This is one reason why African countries are driving regional integration to enlarge the consumer markets. In fact, the East Africa Community (EAC) formed a common market in 2010 with a population of over 130 million. This makes it and its member countries – Rwanda, Burundi, Kenya, Uganda, and Tanzania - a market size on par with Nigeria.

Many Emerging Economies

The 70s, 80s, and early 90s signaled a decline in African economies with many becoming virtually bankrupt and indebted to foreign countries and international organizations like the IMF. Now, most of these countries have low debt and are growing well.

For about 15 years (prior to the economic crisis), 17 of the 53 African economies have maintained economic growth at more than 5% per year on average, according to Steve Radelet, author of *Emerging Africa: How 17 African Countries are Leading the Way.*[7] They have also added 3.2% GDP

---

[6] Mahajan, V. (2008). *Africa Rising: How 900 Million African Consumers Offer More than You Think.* New Jersey: Pearson Prentice Hall.
[7] Radelet, S. (2010). *Emerging Africa: How 17 African Countries are Leading the Way.* Washington, DC: Center for Global Development. (You can also listen to an interview conducted by Lauri Elliott with Steve Radelet at

per capita per year. Some of these countries are Kenya, Mozambique, Tanzania, Uganda, and Ghana.

Ghana is an excellent example of the progress. It became a middle-income country in 2010. Also, it is on target to halve its poverty level by the end of 2015 in line with its Millennium Development Goals (MDGs).

Radelet notes that another six economies, such as Liberia and Sierra Leone, are headed to emerging economy status.

Conclusion

The opening of the 21st century has proved to be a period of shifting paradigms for Africa. It is hard for people to imagine, even with this data, that Africa is any different than what is negatively portrayed in the media.

But the good news is as we speak to people one by one, sharing the new reality, we see the amazement and mental calculations going on their heads. We know this will lead, in many cases, to altering perceptions of the continent.

While there is progress in the battle on many fronts, we still have very steep hills to climb not only as evangelists for Africa but in architects and implementers, making sure that the vision we speak of for the continent comes to fruition fully. This is not a task for a few, but for all of us.

---

http://www.blogtalkradio.com/afribiz/2010/10/07/emerging-economies-in-africa-on-the-rise.)

2

The Future of Africa in 2050

Lauri Elliott

People may acknowledge that Africa has certainly made great strides in its most recent history. However, the bigger question is whether these changes will continue. This chapter looks at likely scenarios for Africa into the future based on existing and emerging patterns.

Africa's Future in 2050

Thank goodness as I was getting ready to co-write this book, I ran across a monograph being done by the Institute for Security Studies[8] in South Africa called *African Futures 2050*.

I had the distinct pleasure of interviewing Dr. Barry Hughes, Director of the Pardee Center of International Futures at the University of Denver in the United States and a partner on the ISS project. This sub-section reflects our discussion.[9]

Population Boom

It has already been established that Africa has the fastest growing population. This boom will cause Africa to surpass both China's and India's population in 2025, less than 15 years away. The combined populations of Asia, including China and India, will still exceed Africa's, however.

If we look out to the year 2100, one in three people will be of African descent globally, even with the likelihood that fertility rates will continue to

---

[8] http://www.issafrica.org
[9] Listen to the interview at http://www.afribiz.net/content/the-future-of-africa-in-2050.

decrease. Lower rates of mortality and increasing life span also contribute to the growing population on the continent.

Within the continent, the populations of East, West, and Central Africa will grow much faster than North and Southern Africa. In 2050, the populations of East and West Africa are expected to exceed 650 million each.

Large population booms have both advantages and disadvantages, as noted by Dr. Hughes. However, from the business perspective, we should see the opportunity in large, growing consumer markets. Unfortunately, the dialogue on population in Africa still remains on the negatives of poverty and disease instead of innovative solutions that will solve these problems, uplifting people and creating strong local economies as discussed in the article, *The Business Proposition of Africa's Population Boom: Problem or Potential?*[10]

In fact, Dr. Hughes notes that the "demographic dividend" is starting to pay off for Africa. The demographic dividend is the portion of people in the labor force of a country. Historically, Africa has been disadvantaged because most of its people were under the age of 15 years. For example, the number of people in the workforce in Africa currently is around 55% compared to about 70% in China, creating a drag on countries.

This is changing as these young populations are maturing. By the middle of the century, 62%-65% of Africa's population will be in the workforce while the percentage of China's population in the workforce will fall well below that as its population ages, according to Dr. Hughes.

This potential workforce will give Africa a distinct advantage globally, but also requires governments and private sector to proactively address the need for jobs sufficiently to provide sustainable livelihoods. Like many countries globally, this issue is already being felt by African nations requiring new innovative solutions to this growing need.

---

[10] Elliott, L. (December 13, 2009). The Business Proposition of Africa's Population Boom: Problem or Potential. *Afribiz.info*. Located online at http://www.afribiz.info/content/the-business-proposition-of-africas-population-boom-a-problem-or-potential.

These demographic dynamics also help us to understand other trends for Africa.

Urbanization

As Africa's population grows, it will also have an impact on cities. Currently, only about 40% of Africa's population resides in urban centers compared to Western regions where the percentages go above 60%. However, the urbanization growth rate in Africa will grow rapidly. This will be a key dynamic to Africa's economic transformation, according to Dr. Hughes. It is also one trend which we consider to be major and to which we dedicate a chapter (*Chapter 5: Urban Centers*) in this book.

As the populations in urban centers grow, more densely populated consumer markets appear, driving more business to the cities and increasing economic activity. These urban agglomerations tend to drive more economic growth than rural areas within nations.

Literacy and Health

Africa will likely not reach its primary education goals by 2015 as outlined in the Millennium Development Goals (MDGs). However, the MDGs have created an impetus for governments to focus attention on this area so that while the literacy rate for the entire continent is somewhere around 68% this should rise to over 90% by 2050.

It's interesting to note that Africa's current literacy rate is comparable to India's, which is considered one of the BRIC emerging markets. So, while literacy is important to a well-trained workforce, participation in the information age, and long-term economic growth, in the immediate future the lack of literacy does not necessarily eliminate economic growth. As Dr. Hughes suggested, people do not necessarily need to be literate to purchase.

On the health front, the key issues are HIV/AIDs and communicable diseases like malaria at this point. It looks like there has been a positive turning point with the number of people dying from or contracting the HIV/AIDs virus going down. However, there is still a lot of uncertainty in this area.

With communicable diseases, there also seems to be progress in terms of the rate in cases of communicable disease, although when looking at just the actual number of cases of communicable disease this may not be reflected. It appears that communicable diseases are rising because of the rapid rise in population.

However, when dividing the number of cases against the larger populations, the rate of new cases of communicable diseases has slowed. Improvements in water and sanitation, as well as malaria nets and other solutions, seem to be producing results.

As these issues become contained, there will be a shift to, or rise in, chronic diseases like diabetes, heart, and cancer. By 2025, the number of deaths from chronic diseases should exceed that of communicable diseases, particularly as the population ages. This will be a dramatic shift in the health care market in Africa. This trend is seen even in South Africa now, for example, with the rise in the rate of obesity and diabetes as the people move up the socioeconomic scale.

Economic Transformation

It's important to look at the diversity of economies when forecasting economic growth. Historically, and even currently, most African economies are reliant upon primary sectors involving commodities, e.g., agriculture, oil.

The *Lions on the Move: The Progress and Potential of African Economies*[11] report, by the McKinsey Global Institute, notes the dynamics of African countries where they have been able to diversify into manufacturing and services and where these sectors exceed 60% of GDP. South Africa and Mauritius are among these countries. Dr. Hughes says that this has allowed countries to enhance exports, but notes that oil exporter countries, e.g., Nigeria, Angola, will likely find this transformation difficult.

---

[11] McKinsey Global Institute. (2010). Lions on the Move: The Progress and Potential of African Economies. Accessed online at http://www.mckinsey.com/mgi/publications/progress_and_potential_of_african_ec onomies/pdfs/MGI_african_economies_full_report.pdf (January 11, 2011).

Diversification is also important in the creation of jobs, particularly for oil exporting countries, as the oil industry does not necessarily create broad opportunities for new jobs itself. Ghana, a new oil producer, is fortunate that its economy is already relatively diversified.

According to Dr. Hughes by 2050, more countries, e.g., Kenya, Nigeria, and Ethiopia, are expected to diversify in excess of 60%. While the process for diversification will have irregular patterns across the continent, it is something that countries will have to reach. So, this is a key economic trend to watch.

Another trend is that economic growth has accelerated across Africa in the last decade with growth rates between 5%-5.5%, exceeding population rates. If Africa keeps this pace, per capita income will increase moving forward.

Regionally, North and Southern Africa's GDP will remain significantly higher than East, West, and Central Africa into 2050. This also is the case for diversification.

Agriculture and Infrastructure

Africa's productivity in agriculture has not made much progress in the last few decades. Production has risen but as a result of more land being used for cultivation rather than higher yields. This is in sharp contrast to developed and developing regions like South America and Asia. So, there is still a big question mark as to what will happen with agriculture.

Dr. Hughes mentioned that there will, however in all likelihood, be an impetus to reverse this trend. We can see evidence of this in the commitment of African countries in the African Union to set aside 10% of their budgets for agriculture, as well as successful agricultural programs in Malawi and Zambia.

Also, Africa is getting assistance from countries, which have been successful in this arena, like Brazil. A report[12] in The Economist documents

---

[12] (August 26, 2010). Brazil's Agricultural Miracle: How to Feed the World. *The Economist*. Located online at http://www.economist.com/node/16889019.

the success of agricultural programs in Brazil over the last few decades in a region with land characteristics similar to Africa. This success is being passed along through programs like the Africa-Brazil Agriculture Innovation Marketplace.[13]

On the infrastructure side, this has been lacking and has hindered growth with the exception of Information Communication Technologies (ICT). Dr. Hughes indicated that the energy capacity in Africa is well below that seen in other developing regions, but we can anticipate a strong push to resolve.

Governance and Conflicts

There has been an increase on the emphasis on elections with more free and fair elections and peaceful transitions in Africa. This excludes the recent examples of Cote d'Ivoire (Ivory Coast) and Libya.

Interestingly enough, Dr. Hughes noted that the exception to the transition to more democratic governments was the North Africa region. He anticipated that as leaders in the region got older and people moved up the socioeconomic scale that there would be a greater push, hopefully peaceful, for reform.

And finally, there are fewer conflicts which will facilitate both improvement in governance and economic growth. In fact, all three feed each other. Because of improvements in all dimensions, there is a virtuous cycle which will propel the continent forward.

Networked World, New Generation, and Complexity

One area of research and specialization for me is looking at how complex systems, networks, and people work. The importance of this arena is becoming more apparent as our world is visibly becoming more complex and chaotic.

When most people hear "networked" world, they think of the Internet and the online environment. This is one aspect. Technology has certainly

---

[13] http://www.africa-brazil.org/

opened the doors for a broader number of people to be involved in society. Its availability and continuing lower costs have helped to push transformation in society. A recent example in Africa is the possible impact of Wikileaks documents in the tipping point for Tunisian and Egyptian government transformation.

However, the technology we speak of is an enabler, which accelerates tipping points. The technology is not the source of the change, but existing and emerging patterns are.

When we speak of emerging patterns[14], we are speaking of patterns that are coming forth in a system although they may not be evident to the majority. Concerning the Egyptian uprising, there were several reports questioning whether U.S. Intelligence had any idea that such an event would occur, catching the U.S. government by surprise.[15] I actually find that amazing when all the signs, or signals, were there. In reality, they probably already knew the likelihood of such events, but not precisely when or where they would occur.

So, what are the emerging patterns surrounding this North Africa transformation? And, what do they have to do with understanding the dynamics of the future of Africa?

First, we are seeing a new generation arise that was not directly touched by the events of the 1950s, 60s, and 70s globally. They have a different outlook on life and different expectations, although fundamentally they want the same things as most people – opportunities, economic prosperity, well-being, etc. They tend to not like the confines of strong control and hierarchical systems whether political, social, or economic.

---

[14] To learn more about emerging patterns and implications for business, read *A Recipe for Change: Emerging Business Patterns* at
http://www.afribiz.net/content/a-recipe-for-change-emerging-business-patterns.
[15] Martin, R. (February 5, 2011). Egypt Unrest: Didn't U.S. Intelligence See It Coming? *NPR*. Accessed online at
http://www.google.com/hostednews/afp/article/ALeqM5i4URLBnwqSuNdzQiJLwJ
noLJSX2A?docId=CNG.ca75d68733ba56c6dff1582ac6bf480a.8a1 (February 6, 2011).

Second, people of this generation are increasingly comfortable with technology and participating online. They are experiencing the opportunity to be their unique selves, at least online, while also experiencing the power of being one voice being connected with many voices.

Third, like the 1960s generation that revolted against the formal institutions of their parents' generation, this generation is doing the same and will continue to do so. This is a natural pattern in human society. Don't get alarmed by the word "revolt". Here it simply means that they are going to force change.

Fourth, this generation is gaining more social, political, and economic power as the young people become the workforce of today and tomorrow. The majority of this generation will be found in developing regions like Asia, Africa, and South America.

Fifth, this generation will be quite adept at handling fluid versus formal organizational structures, which will help them adapt to the complexity inherent in our world. In general, this is not a skill our older generations possess and why many of today's institutions feel overwhelmed by what is happening globally.

The context for much of this generation, which is predominately in developing countries, is high unemployment, disenfranchisement, poverty, and varying degrees of repression, if not oppression. But many of our youth experience some of these issues in almost any country.

This context and the changing aspirations of the new generation[16] are definite signals that suggest problems for existing, formal structures that do not adapt to the new reality. In fact, the U.S. and other countries are aware of the problem and have been for a while. That's why recently, at the World Economic Forum, global business leaders called for inclusive growth.

We can see how the elements of the networked world, complexity, and the new generation converge in the story of Wael Ghonim, who is an

---

[16] To learn more about this new generation from a consumer perspective, read *The Age of Identity and the Facebook Generation* at http://www.afribiz.net/content/the-age-of-identity-and-the-facebook-generation.

Egyptian, a Google executive in the Middle East, and young. He was credited with helping to catalyze the Egyptian protests through Facebook.

Ghonim is obviously well educated and traveled. He has maintained that the protests were not political mechanizations from foreign powers, but born out of the heart of the Egyptian people - a people who constitute the second largest population in Africa and is young.

So, as the networked world continues, the new generation rises, and complexity abounds, what does that mean for Africa's future? It will definitely be a different, but positive experience if we can grasp the patterns and ride the waves.

In the *African Futures 2050* monograph, it describes this environment very well – dispersed global power and greater independence. First, dispersed global power means that there will be power distributed more broadly across the globe. From a national perspective, we see that already happening with the rise of China and India. However, these power regimes will not just be dispersed differently among national governments, but also with informal and fluid networks.

Second, the interdependence will come through areas like trade and economic growth, energy, and climate change. Over the last several years, I have spent time looking at emerging patterns in which our world systems would begin to reflect more of our natural, complex systems. This means they would transform from domination or control structures to interdependence systems, which require new ways of organizing, working, and communicating.

The impact of these two environmental trends and Africa's position in this context are discussed in more detail in *Chapter 3: Africa's Business and Geopolitical Rise.* The crux for business is to learn new ways of shaping strategy and operations to be successful in this new context, particularly in Africa.

Conclusion

Not only has Africa demonstrated positive progress in the past few decades on many fronts, the current patterns suggest that this progress will continue into 2050. An understanding of these patterns help businesses understand the context in which they will operate, including opportunities and challenges.

These patterns also suggest that how business is conducted in Africa needs to change. The potential of Africa is not only in its natural resources, but also in its growing population, among other things. If businesses plan to tap these opportunities, they will need to re-think and adapt for these patterns, and others, going forward.

3

Africa's Business and Geopolitical Rise

Lauri Elliott

While the global economic crisis was by no means easy on Africa, it did allow the veil over Africa to be drawn away to show what has been waiting to be discovered on the continent. While the world sat in darkness, Africa became a great light. As the world seeks more and more new markets, rich with both natural resources and large, growing consumer markets, Africa's star will rise.

Africa as an Epicenter of Global Trade

After the G20 meetings in Toronto in June 2010, it was very clear nations see a new era of a multi-polar world. Fareed Zakaria, host of CNN's GPS and author of *The Post-American World*[17], applied the concept of a multi-polar world to politics, or nation states. In essence, the world agenda will no longer be dominated by one or a few nations. Political power will be dispersed more broadly.

In a report by Accenture called *The Rise of the Multi-Polar World*[18], it says that global economic power will no longer reside with the United States, Europe, and Japan. It will disperse as "developing economies contribute an ever-increasing share of the world's output, trade and investment." In fact, developing countries are expected to account for two-

---

[17] Zakaria, F. (2009). *The Post-American World.* New York, NY: W.W. Norton & Company.
[18] Accenture. (2007). The Rise of the Multi-Polar World.

thirds of global trade in 2050, according to *The World Order in 2050*[19] policy outlook by Uri Dadush and Bennett Stancil.

In the backdrop of these dynamics, seemingly, is Africa. With little representation in the G20, reduced votes in the International Monetary Fund, and perhaps not enough impact in other international organizations like the United Nations and World Health Organization, it would seem Africa is a loser in this new era.

But political and economic dynamics are not the only things changing. Forms of influence and power are also changing. Power is also dispersing among spheres of society, who are interconnected. The most common spheres are business, social, and government. However, today these spheres are overlaid with transnational networks, global policy networks, advocacy networks, value networks, social networks gone viral, etc. This will result in influence and power emerging in new and different forms, allowing more diverse and unique ways of articulating and acting upon influence and power.

While Africa may seem to be losing ground in some formal arenas, it may have gained ground where it matters – economics. And because new and different forms of influence and power are emerging, Africa will be able to find ways to leverage its growing economic influence.

The shape of Africa's growing economic influence is centered on two areas – being a pole of growth and an epicenter of trade. With solid economic performance, abundant natural resources, and a large consumer market, Africa is on a path to be one of the poles, or regions, of growth in spite of Sub-Saharan Africa having the predominate number of Least Developed Countries (LDCs).

The other area in Africa's growing economic influence has not been clearly articulated or stressed. Africa is positioned as an epicenter and gateway for global business and trade. This has quietly snuck up on the world while the world was focused on the economic crisis.

---

[19] Dadush, U., & Stancil, B. (2010). The World Order in 2050. *Policy Outlook.* Carnegie Endowment for International Peace.

If you look at the number of trade agreements being introduced between Africa and the rest of the world at this time (e.g., between the United States and Angola, between China and many African states, between India, Brazil, and South Africa), you will see that they are increasing and expanding. In the last few years, heads of states from around the world, e.g., Iran, Russia, Brazil, United States, France, have visited Africa to improve diplomatic and economic ties.

These activities do not occur unless there are significant benefits sought by these nations. It's obvious that Africa has something the world wants. During the Cold War era, Africa served as a geopolitical map of opposing political ideologies between the U.S. and Soviet Union. But now, the primary focus is economic because strong economies bolster governments, those in office, communities, and citizens. This is not to ignore other benefits that countries might seek, like cultural exchange, from ties with African nations.

Also, there is increased south south and developing country cooperation, which means trade and business flows are moving in new directions. The developing economies that will lead global trade in 2050 are increasingly trading among themselves, but not to the exclusion of developed countries. In this, Africa is increasingly part of the engagement. Look at the India, Brazil, South Africa (IBSA) Forum activities, the China-Africa Forum activities, and the Southern African Customs Union's (SACU) preferential trade agreement with the Southern Common Market (MERCOSUR) as examples.

In this context, Africa's rising economic influence will translate to more political influence, which may be "soft" more than formal in the short-to-medium term. For example, Nicolas Sarkozy, President of France, held the 25th annual Africa-France Summit in 2010, which focused not on politics but on business. At the summit, Sarkozy said he would call for an expanded role of African nations in the United Nations when he heads the G20 this year. And also, Canadian Prime Minister Stephen Harper personally invited additional African leaders like President Goodluck Jonathan of Nigeria and African Union Chairperson Bingu wa Mutharika to attend the G20 Toronto Summit in 2010 in recognition of the need to include the region.

But another primary benefit of these political and economic processes is that Africa will serve as a global trade epicenter and gateway into other emerging markets, and even into developed nations. Africa has the ability to be a bridge to enter into other markets, as well as a key location for global value chains.

U.S. Honeywell has taken its Chinese connections to enter the Sub-Saharan African market, so why couldn't firms use Africa to enter other regions because of Africa's increasingly favorable ties? In another instance, Chinese firms are partnering with African governments to establish economic zones and manufacturing capacity in Africa based on the experience of economic zones in China. This will create capacity for these firms to serve China's domestic market and the African consumer markets in the future.

And finally, a question that comes to mind is "How well is Africa positioned to be an epicenter and gateway of global trade?" Africa still faces many hard realities like poverty, lack of infrastructure, unemployment, and instability in some countries, but other developing nations also face the same or similar issues. And, for the most part, African countries have proven to be economically and politically resistant to instability in the last decade. Governance and the business climate have also improved while conflicts have reduced dramatically.

But in truth, Africa does not need everything in place, but it does need enough significant leverage points to take advantage of this position and use them to create a tipping point to solidly establish and maintain this position. As indicated before, the increasing diplomatic and economic ties between Africa and the rest of the world, its natural resources, and large, growing consumer markets are key leverage points.

Another leverage point is the image of Africa, which is changing. The successful conclusion of the FIFA World Cup in South Africa perhaps helped to produce a tipping point.

And one leverage point not used enough is that there are pockets in Africa, South Africa and Mauritius for example, where business is run on par, in many facets, with the world. In fact, there are many more places where this is the case because of economic zones. An economic zone, such as a free trade zone or export–processing zone, generally has a good climate, procedures, infrastructure, business support, laws, and incentives conducive for business, even when the country in which it is located does not. And if you dig a little deeper, you will find more significant leverage points.

A Look at South Africa's Recent Strategic Moves

2010 was a major year for South Africa with the successful FIFA World Cup. However significant the event, it pales in comparison to the global political positioning South Africa has worked for itself in the past year. It is obvious the government continues to learn more about how to use the country's strategic, not just natural, assets to secure its position globally. Hopefully, this will help South Africa economically in the future.

In 2010, President Zuma visited each of the BRIC (Brazil, Russia, India, and China) countries to cement and increase both political and economic ties. The recent result is South Africa being approved as a member by BRIC member nations, so effectively BRIC becomes BRICS.

It's also important to remember what BRIC actually represents. In *The World Needs Better Economic BRICs*[20], Jim O'Neill of Goldman Sachs coined the phrase, BRIC, referring to the countries in terms of their advancing stage of economic development as emerging economies. Goldman Sachs projects they may economically overtake the richest nations by 2050. China has already headed down this path by overtaking Japan and Germany in the last year to rank as the world's 2nd largest economy.

Goldman Sachs has more recently presented a second series of nations it believes will arise called N11, including Egypt, Nigeria, and Vietnam. South Africa does not appear on either of Goldman Sachs' lists.

South Africa does appear on two other emerging economies lists – CIVETS (Colombia, Indonesia, Vietnam, Egypt, Turkey, and South Africa) and MAVINS (Mexico, Australia, Vietnam, Indonesia, Nigeria, and South Africa). So, there is recognition of potential but what remains at issue is

---

[20] O'Neill, J. (2001). The World Needs Better Economic BRICS. *Global Economics: Paper No. 66.* Goldman Sachs. Available online at http://www2.goldmansachs.com/ideas/brics/building-better-doc.pdf.

how will South Africa continue to progress for the long term when its medium-term economic prospects are sluggish?

Even though O'Neill says that South Africa is not the best choice for the next BRIC because of the size of its consumer market and struggling economy, it was chosen anyway by the current BRIC. How is that? South Africa has become better at leveraging its assets strategically and being a BRIC is no longer just about economics but also geopolitics.

While these designations - BRIC, N11, CIVETS, and MAVIN - are only descriptors and do not represent any formal economic bloc, the BRIC nations have formed an alliance to increase their geopolitical influence seeing as they already represent more than half the world's global growth. Accepting South Africa as a BRIC, demonstrates the importance the BRICs place on Africa going into the future and possibly South Africa's ability to help further ties with the rest of the continent. So, South Africa has been accepted geopolitically, but not necessarily economically, as a BRIC. This occurrence aligns with the insights shared previously about Africa's new position as a global business, trade, and investment hub.

South Africa is also a member of the G20 nations, which are supposed to work together to coordinate policies that impact global economics. In 2011, South Africa will take a two-year, non-permanent member rotation on the UN Security Council, effectively replacing Uganda which has held a position for the last two years. And it is likely that South Africa will gain more votes in the International Monetary Fund within the next two years as the IMF shifts 6% more voting power to emerging markets.

Along with still being the largest economy in Africa, these dynamics will no doubt give South Africa the ability to yield more of what U.S. Secretary of State Clinton calls "smart power". But what South Africa needs out of this more than anything else is the economic benefit.

South Africa's trade with the United States and European Union combined still exceeds over 30%, although China as a country is now the largest trade partner with South Africa. Economic recovery in the U.S. and Europe is expected to slow in 2011, and South Africa's economic recovery is expected to slow as well. In essence, South Africa does not expect to experience broad-based growth, which the IMF projects for Sub-Saharan Africa in 2011.

While there are many reasons South Africa would seek strong ties with the existing BRICs, the fact that at least India and China are expected to have strong growth rates over the next few years presents an opportunity for stimulating South Africa's economy through trade with the existing BRICs. In the long run, the BRIC consumer markets present increased opportunities just on sheer size. South Africa has the smallest consumer market of the soon-to-be BRICS alliance with approximately 50 million people. This compares to approximately 139 million people in Russia, 200 million people in Brazil, 1.1 billion people in India, and 1.3 billion in China.[21]

Even with economic struggles, South Africa is still an emerging economy and the BRICS designation will help the country continue to transform its brand image positively. South Africa will also find preferential trade status within BRICS, which was already well underway and opens more doors for South African businesses and investors.

And finally, South Africa represents the strongest formal flows of information, resources, investment, trade, and business on the continent. If you operate or have strong partnerships in South Africa, it opens doors to south south trade flows not just north south trade flows. And it's the south south and African regional trade flows that will become increasingly important over the next few decades.

Conclusion

As we have seen the rise of China in both the economic and political spheres, particularly in the last decade, Africa will also rise. However, the forms of Africa's power and influence over the next decades still remain to be seen.

---

[21] Central Intelligence Agency. (2010). *The World Factbook.* Accessed online at https://www.cia.gov/library/publications/the-world-factbook/index.html (December 2010).

It's important for everyone involved with Africa to realign their mindsets with Africa's new position. Otherwise, Africa can be destined to a repeat of history.

Remember, Africa has its own inherent assets, power, and influence with over 50 sovereign states and over 1 billion people. It and its people are endowed with natural resources – oil, minerals, land, water, etc. – that the world demands. There also is a rich tapestry of culture, innovation, knowledge, wisdom, and talent coming from its people on the continent and in the diaspora.

As an African American, I can say that more and more African people, nations, and advocates need to speak, operate, and negotiate out of Africa's position, potential, and strengths. We can only expect others to see Africa as an asset if we do.

4

Shifting Mindsets and Strategies about Africa

Lauri Elliott

Nissi Ekpott

In the last few years, we have seen attitudes towards Africa change more positively, but there is still a lot of work to be done. It is not sufficient until there is a critical mass of people and organizations, both inside and outside of the continent, which shift their mindsets and strategies regarding Africa.

This chapter pulls together thoughts and directions Nissi and I have synthesized over the past few years. These are points we often raise in public forums, hoping that the fire that shines so brightly in Africa will catch on. And we know that we are not alone in some of these views.

What We Can Learn from Obama's Ghana Speech

Obama spoke at the Ghanaian Parliament during his first trip to Sub-Saharan Africa as President in July 2009. He used this forum to imprint his administration's perspectives and priorities for U.S.-Africa relations. While some people may argue about motives behind the words and the accuracy of statements, the speech does reveal a needed paradigm shift with how the world does business with Africa.

First, interact with Africa with purpose. In choosing Ghana, Obama highlighted an African nation striving for values complementary to the United States, and one which his administration would support through its foreign assistance framework. Having purpose provides focus, allowing the placement of assets and resources where they will provide strategic benefit.

Second, be a partner to Africa instead of a patron. Much of the world still patronizes Africa. Yet, there are over 50 sovereign states in which business is conducted every day. As partners with Africans, we recognize that Africans drive and are responsible for their own destiny. Such partnerships would, as Obama said, "...be grounded in mutual responsibility and mutual respect."

Third, recognize Africa as a serious player in the global economy instead of as a bystander. Obama put it this way:

> *"This is the simple truth of a time when the boundaries between people are overwhelmed by our connections. Your prosperity can expand America's prosperity. Your health and security can contribute to the world's health and security. And the strength of your democracy can help advance human rights for people everywhere."*

In a nutshell, what happens in Africa affects the world. What happens across the globe affects Africa.

Fourth, see the prosperity that exists in Africa. As noted in both Time and the Harvard Business Review, doing business and investing in Africa are among the best ideas for 2009. In fact, Africa has provided better returns on investment than other global regions in the last several years.

Obama also sees this prosperity extending to the broader African society – a key to eliminating poverty. He said:

> *"With better governance, I have no doubt that Africa holds the promise of a broader base of prosperity. Witness the extraordinary success of Africans in my country, America. They're doing very well. So they've got the talent, they've got the entrepreneurial spirit. The question is, how do we make sure that they're succeeding here in their home countries? The continent is rich in natural resources. And from cell phone entrepreneurs to small farmers, Africans have shown the capacity and commitment to create their own opportunities."*

In essence, Africa is a place of prosperity instead of poverty with the right frameworks in place.

Fifth, strive for trade and investment over aid. Obama indicates an understanding that more trade will benefit both Africa and America:

> *"Now, America can also do more to promote trade and investment. Wealthy nations must open our doors to goods and services from Africa in a meaningful way. That will be a commitment of my administration. And where there is good governance, we can broaden prosperity through public-private partnerships that invest in better roads and electricity; capacity-building that trains people to grow a business; financial services that reach not just the cities but also the poor and rural areas. This is also in our own interests — for if people are lifted out of poverty and wealth is created in Africa, guess what? New markets will open up for our own goods. So it's good for both."*

There is only so much that the old cycle of aid can do. Trade opens the door for growth.

Sixth, adapt process and protocol to the African context. Obama is known for his use of social media to connect with U.S. citizens. However, the landscape for media in Africa is different. Recognizing this, the Obama team incorporated a radio broadcast, simulcast the speech to U.S. embassies across the African continent, delivered highlights of his speech via SMS, and used the popular African social media platform, MXIT, to interact with Africans.

And finally, all parties need to learn from the past but not live in the past. While Africa has experienced trouble in the last century, Kofi Annan said at the 2009 World Economic Forum on Africa that "Africa has transformed in my lifetime and the progress reached so far is proof that concrete achievements are possible amidst adversity."

But even with this progress, many know that Africa still has not fulfilled its promise. Obama re-ignites the hope held in this promise when he said:

> *"So I believe that this moment is just as promising for Ghana and for Africa as the moment when my father came of age and new*

nations were being born. This is a new moment of great promise. Only this time, we've learned that it will not be giants like Nkrumah and Kenyatta who will determine Africa's future. Instead, it will be you – the men and women in Ghana's parliament (and) the people you represent. It will be the young people brimming with talent and energy and hope who can claim the future that so many in previous generations never realized."

This crucial time in global history provides an opportunity for the world to re-adjust its dealings with Africa. Doing so will allow us to get down to business in order to do business – business that will promote both national and global stability and prosperity.

Transforming Our Minds about Doing Business in Africa

Perception has emerged as a powerful influence in today's economic world. Economic activities are highly influenced by perceived risk in a geographic area. It is widely acknowledged that Africa suffers a negative perception of itself and from the view point of foreign investors. Many people have been typically sold a picture of a totally dysfunctional Africa.

Amidst its complexities, Africa offers valid opportunity for investments, vibrant communities, citizens eager for change, a growing market, fast changing laws, a transforming society, etc. It is the next frontier for growth and development. This includes business.

Business is highly influenced by perception also, and hence it is fundamental that the perception towards Africa is addressed as a first step towards doing business on the continent. There are certain long standing paradigms that have dogged the continent. Following is a new frame full of new mindsets.

Help the Poor by Helping the Rich

The current paradigm says that all Africans are poor and desperately need help. Mahajan, author of *Africa Rising*, provides estimates that say there are about 450 million people living below the poverty level. However, Africa has about a billion people. This means there's another 450 to 500 million who can afford goods and services.

Additional estimates shared by Mahajan place the African middle class at about 150 million people, who are able to purchase goods at par with the rest of the world. This is equivalent to India's middle class. Focus needs to be placed on growing the wealthier 450 million as a strategy towards lifting the poorer 450 million out of poverty.

This new shift will create a virtuous cycle, i.e., invest in businesses that provide goods and services for the wealthier 450 million, thus creating jobs for the lower 450 million. These 450 million people will eventually move up the economic scale, demanding and able to afford more goods and services.

This model is similar to what has happened in China over the past twenty to thirty years, creating the world's biggest economic upliftment. This moved hundreds of millions of people from poverty.

Reduce Poverty through Small Business

The current paradigm says that creating enterprise is not as important as aid. Fortunately, we are on the nexus of this paradigm shift.

African poverty can be greatly reduced through micro, small, and medium enterprises (SMMEs). These are the engines of economic growth for countries globally. Small businesses create more jobs than any other entity. Because of the African communal lifestyle, every single job created through small businesses affects at least four lives. In some African contexts, the ratio is greater.

A Transformed Purpose for Aid

Aid, on its own, cannot eradicate poverty. Aid should be an emergency measure targeted especially at severe, distressed sectors. It should also focus on sectors which do not easily and immediately attract investors. However, it should not become a permanent feature.

Also, donor agencies, aid agencies, and mission organizations need to actively re-tool their model towards Africa. They should channel at least 25% of their funding into sustainable business investments. They can still be focused on the communities in which they serve.

Transfer Responsibility

The current paradigm is that Africa cannot solve its problems, and is perpetually dependent on foreign solutions. In actuality, Africa can solve most of its problems internally. Where foreign aid organizations bring help, it should be complementary.

Such bodies and agencies should target turning their current recipients into donors within a ten-year period. Repeating this process will subsequently reduce poverty and transfer the responsibility of wealth creation squarely into the hands of Africans themselves.

Africans Themselves Want Change

The current paradigm is that Africans are passive and beggarly. However, there is an increasing demand by Africans for trade rather than aid.

This desire is reflected both in the government and private sector. Presidents, like Yoweri Museveni of Uganda, are quoted as requesting more trade, not aid. Paul Kagame, President of Rwanda, has launched a national program to shift the mindset of his nation away from aid. This mindset is increasingly spreading across the continent.

Increased Investment in the Private Sector Improves Governance

The current paradigm is Africa is all about bad governance, and that only a change in governance can change things. This means the focus is on politics and governance.

There is a saying that he who pays the piper dictates the tune. When businesses are empowered, they are able to affect governance in the long run. They become stronger, growing into tax payers and hence influencers. They have a voice and sooner or later government listens to them. For example, the Nigerian government some time ago set up a committee of over 300 of its leading business people to craft business laws aimed at propelling its economy in the next ten years.

On the other hand, when a government's chief source of income is foreign aid, it dances to the tune of foreign donors, which at times is at the expense of its local private sector. It is not motivated to listen to its people.

Business is Already Doing a Lot

The current paradigm is businesses in Africa are only greedy and exploitative. In truth, many successful African businesses have already taken up significant levels of social responsibility, including projects like fighting disease, sponsoring education, and developing community projects.

Through these companies, many have received aid from local sources. In a Lesotho clothing factory, staff has its maternity and other hospital needs covered by clinics sponsored by the company. In South Africa, staff is allowed to recommend social projects into which businesses invest. In some parts of the continent, companies send out staff to help in community projects like building houses. These examples help prove that businesses play a huge role in solving problems.

Africa Offers Unlimited Business Opportunities

The current paradigm is there are few profitable opportunities in Africa. Actually, almost every type of business operating in Africa shows profitability. Because most African countries have low development thresholds, there is huge demand in almost every sector. This is unlike many Western markets, which have become saturated.

There is Money to be Made

The current paradigm is there is no money to be made. People are poor and cannot afford goods and services.

In fact, many African countries benefited from the resource boom of the last few years, before the collapse of 2008. Many of these are awash with cash.

For example, Nigeria drove its foreign reserves from $7 billion in 2001 to about $63 billion in 2008. Today, those reserves are at about $33 billion. The country is planning to set up a sovereign wealth fund with a view to finding lucrative opportunities to invest its wealth.

African countries need help to avoid capital flight by helping communities produce most of their consumer needs, such as food, clothing, and housing. These are only more opportunities for entrepreneurs.

There is Risk Involved, but a Commensurate High Rate of Return

The current paradigm is that Africa is simply too risky. Its political tensions at times, weak judicial systems, and certain unstable societies seem not to offer any attraction to some investors. However, the truth is that the return on investment in Africa far outstrips what is possible from most other regions. Many people refer to these returns as a "well-hidden" secret that has been beneficial to a few business people.

Africa has its risks, and they abound. Businesses open up and shut down for one reason or the other. This is not exclusive to Africa. The global business failure rate is not far different from what it is in Africa.

Conclusion

There are several new, or shifting, mindsets that have been presented here. They are seeds that have been planted, hopefully, in the good soil of your mind. But as with any seed, these new mindsets need to be cultivated – mulled over, discussed, and acted upon.

While we are thankful that you have picked up our book to read, we want to be honest here. We didn't write this book for people to be more informed. We wrote it for people to take action.

Edward Burke said the famous words, "All that is necessary for the triumph of evil is for good men to do nothing." One definition for evil is "causing harm".[22] Evil, in this case, is letting untapped potential and promise go to waste. Evil is letting prosperity bypass people when it is within reach. The harm, or evil, that exists regarding Africa is in a great part because we allow it to remain.

Africa should be a place of prosperity for its own, as well as the world. We each have the power within our spheres of control and influence to make it so.

---

[22] http://www.m-w.com

Selected Markets
and Sectors

5

Urban Centers

Hartmut Sieper

Urbanization is one of the big megatrends in the world of today and tomorrow. Millions of people are migrating from rural to urban areas for many reasons. While the percentage of people living in urban areas has already reached very high levels in the Western world and Latin America, some parts of Asia and most parts of Africa are lagging behind.

The urban population in Africa accounts for about 40% of the continent's total population. In Latin America, a similar proportion between urban and rural population was observed in 1950. Within the next decade, more than 80% of all Latin Americans will live in cities.[23] So, Africa lies 60 years behind Latin America if it follows the same trajectory.

The urban population growth in Africa is mainly determined by two major factors: the migration of mostly young people from rural to urban areas, and high general population growth because of high fertility rates and low median ages. And because Africa's youth bulge is now reaching adulthood and will move to cities for better opportunities, Africa will quickly catch up with Latin America.

Strongest Urban Population Growth in Africa

According to UN-HABITAT, Africa will experience the strongest growth among all regions of the world until 2050. From 2000 to 2030, Africa's urban population will grow from 294 million to 742 million people, an

---

[23] UN-HABITAT. (2010). The State of African Cities 2010: Governance, Inequalities and Urban Land Markets. Accessed online at http://www.unhabitat.org/documents/SACR-ALL-10-FINAL.pdf (January 8, 2011).

increase of 152%. In comparison, the urban population in Asia will grow by 94% while Latin America will grow by 55%.

The three largest cities in Africa are Cairo (Egypt), Lagos (Nigeria), and Kinshasa (DRC).[24] Cairo and Lagos populations exceed 10 million, making them megacities. The following image shows the largest and fastest growing cities in Africa.

Source: Trans Africa Invest, based on data of CityMayors

---

[24] In other sources, Johannesburg, South Africa is in the top largest cities in Africa because the East Rand is incorporated into the figures. The UN-HABITAT figures here separate the two.

In about 10 years, Cairo will be overtaken by Lagos and Kinshasa. Many African cities will have grown more than 50% between 2006 and 2020.

Another factor influencing urbanization is how densely populated a country is. The small country of Rwanda has already passed levels of sustainability regarding the ability to feed their own people with agricultural goods from local sources.

Too many people are living too close to each other, allowing only very small parcels of agricultural land per family. Fertile ground in this country is almost 100% utilized, so that there is no further expansion possible. As a result of this unpleasant situation, many young people are forced to leave their parents' farms and move into the cities looking for a job, or any informal business activity, that will allow them to earn a living.

Urbanization will definitely accelerate in countries with this problem. Right now, more than 80% of the overall population of the East African countries of Rwanda, Burundi, Uganda, and Ethiopia is still living in rural areas. Consequently, rapid growth of the primary cities of these countries can be anticipated with very high probability.

Uganda is an excellent example for the extreme dynamics of future urban growth. The country has one of the youngest populations worldwide. Regarding fertility (6.73 children born per woman) and birthrate (47.55 births /1,000 population), Uganda is ranked second, according to the *World Factbook*. The population growth rate is approximately 3.6% per year, according to 2010 estimates. The median age is 15, which means that half the population is younger than 15 years. One can anticipate the transformation of this high youth population - from too young to being productive citizens; from a burden to a benefit when the majority of youth reach adulthood. What is called the "demographic dividend" will begin to pay off.

One can easily imagine the future exponential growth of urban areas. In 2008, only 13% of Ugandans were living in cities. Over the next 20 years, the urban population will well exceed the 20% level, leading to rapid growth of the capital city of Kampala, which is also the economic and financial center of the country.

The rapid growth of African cities will both imply major problems and create outstanding opportunities. The challenges are obvious. They range from infrastructure gaps and missing capacities for power, water, and food supply to loss of agricultural land and chaotic traffic situations, not to mention the huge health problems originating from air pollution, lack of sanitation, and huge piles of garbage.

Harare, Zimbabwe: Offers good value for investors because of depressed asset prices as a result of the 2009 currency reform and political uncertainties. (Photo by: Hartmut Sieper)

Clever entrepreneurs, who understand problems are also opportunities, will find a large variety of promising business concepts by proactively dealing with the aforementioned challenges in city development in Africa. Sophisticated city planning methods, innovative waste management procedures, cost efficient water treatment technologies, and independent power plants belong to this category of opportunities.

Increasing Land Prices

Studying past history reveals another set of opportunities. When we look back to urban expansion in Western countries, we find some business cases that should work in Africa as well. Land prices will increase when the plots move closer to the city. Many farmers in Europe became millionaires just because their farmland was converted into building land.

From an investor's point of view, we will take a look at some glaring opportunities that are connected with the megatrend of urbanization in Africa. There is a significant unsatisfied need in residential housing in most major African cities. The gap between demand and supply is still increasing, offering numerous opportunities for real estate developers, prefab house suppliers, and construction companies.

In Latin America, households need 5.4 times their annual income to buy a house. In Africa, they need an average of 12.5 times their annual income.[25] If developers can provide more affordable and quality solutions to consumers, there are enormous opportunities.

The market environment is completely different from the situation that we are familiar with in Western economies. An example is if you want to rent a flat in some cities like Lagos, Douala, or Luanda, you have to pay the rent for up to 24 months in advance. For real estate developers, such down payments from future renters will provide a solid base for financing ventures.

However, it is not so easy to tap into this kind of business opportunity. In practical terms, it can be very difficult, costly, and time-consuming to get the necessary licenses for starting operations. Corruption is known to exist. Securing and maintaining ownership rights might also be difficult, depending on the rule of law, the availability and reliability of title deeds, and the handling process in general.

---

[25]http://www.dramatispersonae.org/RealEstateAndDevelopmentFrontPageAffHousingAfrica.htm

The more well developed real estate markets are found in North Africa, including Egypt and Morocco, Cape Verde, and South Africa to name a few. Because they are more developed, rates of return may not be as high though. There are online resources to help decipher the investment and business climate related to land across countries.[26]

In some countries, where there is no private ownership of urban land possible, lease holds can be obtained for a period of 25, 49, or even 99 years. In many countries, leasing is the only possibility of getting agricultural land. Lease rates can be very inexpensive and be negotiated for a long period. This might be very attractive for long-term investors.

Lagos, Nigeria: There is a never-ending construction boom. (Photo by: Hartmut Sieper)

Investors that want to find out which cities would offer the best development perspective and the biggest potential for future price increases would have to look for a number of parameters. The most important factor

---

[26] For example, visit the International Finance Corporation's websites – http://www.investingacrossborders.org and http://www.doingbusiness.org.

is location. This is true for selecting the right strategic location, i.e., in which city the property should be bought, as well as choosing the right quarter within the city. If you intend to buy property outside the big cities in order to benefit from lower prices, there should be a positive outlook for future development.

Rapidly growing cities will accommodate an increasing number of inhabitants, workers, and consumers. If everything goes right, prices should increase and all stakeholders would be able to prosper.

Development Corridors

Another urbanization pathway to consider is development corridors. In Africa, there are 12 key spatial development corridors recognized by the African Union. Another type of corridor, perhaps even sub-sets of the spatial development corridors, are urban development corridors connecting urban centers. Selecting locations along these corridors within a country or across borders is a good idea. Examples of these corridors are:

- Johannesburg/Pretoria – Nelspruit – Maputo
- Johannesburg – Durban
- Johannesburg – Gaborone – Francistown – Bulawayo – Gweru – Kadoma – Harare
- Harare – Mutare – Beira
- Harare – Lusaka – Ndola – Lubumbashi
- Lagos – Porto Novo – Lome – Accra – Takoradi – Abidjan
- Luanda – Kinshasa/Brazzaville – Libreville – Douala
- Douala – Yaounde – Bangui – Ndjamena
- Mombasa – Nairobi – Kampala
- Kampala – Entebbe

Along these major corridors, many business opportunities will emerge. Truckers want to eat and to sleep. Commuters will visit shopping centers. Minibuses will stop at many places along the road. Those highly frequented places are good locations to sell goods and services.

The overland roads carry further business opportunities like public transportation, logistics services, international border controls, and road construction and maintenance. Other opportunities include agricultural estates, food processing plants, and real estate development.

Urban Expansion Patterns

Let us take a look at how bustling cities expand. Lack of opportunities in rural areas where unemployment rates are very high will cause local people to move into the cities, leading to uncontrolled growth. Depending on the local geographical situation, distinct expansion patterns can be observed.

A common pattern is the extension of urban settlements along major routes into the city. Suburbs along primary roads will quickly develop and amalgamate with the expanding city. For example, the suburbs of Oduponkpehe, Ashiaman, and Tema are now included in the Greater Accra area.

Cities that have natural, or political, boundaries in one or two directions will have to expand into the remaining directions. A good example is Kinshasa, DRC. It can only expand to the south and to the west. To the north, Brazzaville and the Congo River are its natural limits. To the east, there is a big swamp. A logical consequence is higher population density in the inner city, as well as rapidly increasing prices for land and rentals.

Eko Atlantic City, Lagos, Nigeria: The new dynamic city on a reclamated piece of land will house 250,000 residents. (Source: www.ekoatlantic.com)

Lagos, the huge mega city in the southwest corner of Nigeria has its own problems. Downtown Lagos stretches over four islands that are connected by long bridges, leading to a very difficult traffic situation. Expansion seems to be possible only on the mainland. However, Nigeria and city planners have developed the compelling project of building a new quarter on new land, which has to be reclaimed from the sea. According to this ambitious plan, Eko Atlantic City will become the new financial district of Lagos, located south of Victoria Island. Reclamation activities have already begun.

Eko Atlantic City will be spread across seven districts, combining residential, commercial, financial, and tourist development:

- Development area: over 9 square kilometers
- Land for sale: approximately 6 square kilometers
- Length of city: 7 kilometers
- Average width of city: 1.4 kilometers
- Expected number of buildings: 3,000
- Resident population: 250,000
- Commuters: 150,000
- Length of internal roads: 100 kilometers
- Length of internal waterway: 20 kilometers
- Duration of marine works: 6 years
- Sand for reclamation: 140 million tons
- Number of plots for sale: approximately 1,500 (excluding the Financial District)

The development of this new part of Lagos will create numerous opportunities for business and investment.

Air Traffic Patterns

An interesting question is "Which large cities will benefit most from globalization and intra-regional trade?" We can use air traffic patterns and growth to draw some insights. In Sub-Saharan Africa, the major international airport in Johannesburg, O.R. Tambo, is by far the most frequented one, followed by those in Nairobi and Addis Ababa. In the long term, the importance of Johannesburg should decrease because other destinations like Luanda, Lusaka, and Harare will increase in importance, thus allowing passengers from Europe to get to Angola, Zambia, and Zimbabwe directly instead of transferring at Johannesburg. In West Africa, Lagos and Accra will benefit from new intra West African flight routes.

The future of the international airport in Addis Ababa should be bright. The capital city of Ethiopia, the third most populous African country, is ideally located as a strategic gateway from Asia to Africa. Recognizing this competitive advantage, Ethiopian Airlines has already opened new flight routes from Addis Ababa to China and India. It can be anticipated that Addis Ababa will grow significantly over the next decade since this city is centrally located and, by far, the biggest and most important urbanized area in Ethiopia.

The following air traffic trends can be observed and should remain intact over this decade:

- Western European hubs (Paris, London) will lose importance
- Asian hubs (Dubai, Istanbul) will develop well
- Intra- and inter-regional air traffic in Africa will dramatically increase
- Low-cost airlines will spread, leading to lower cost of transportation

Key Challenges and Business Opportunities

By following the megatrend of urbanization in Africa, there are many sectors where challenges can and should be understood as business opportunities.

Infrastructure

Infrastructure is one of the big challenges in Africa. Almost everything is needed. A high demand meets an unsatisfactory supply, if any. There is a lack of water, electricity, sewage systems, roads, railroads, vehicles, public transportation systems, and many more, creating vast areas of business and investment opportunities.

According to IEA World Energy Outlook[27], 1.4 billion people worldwide lack access to electricity. Electrification percentage rates in some African countries, especially in Central and Eastern Africa are below 10%.

It is still often the case that industrial companies, which want to build manufacturing units somewhere in Africa, must develop independent infrastructure like power, water supply, and road access. This contributes to discouragement of some strategic investors, yet those who do implement, such as Sher Karuturi (a leading producer of roses globally), can find success.

Water Supply

The majority of African people do not have access to clean drinking water. This is especially true for rural areas, where there are virtually no water treatment facilities in place. Even in most of the big cities, tap water is not safe to drink. Therefore, many opportunities arise from the urgent need of people to get access to potable water, as well as to save water. Some of these opportunities are:

- Water treatment technologies, i.e., by purification liquids or tablets, filter systems, desalination systems
- Water transportation systems
- For countries with physically scarce water resources: planning and construction of water retention basins; identification of unused underground water sources; introduction of waterless toilets; and drip irrigation systems

---

[27] http://www.worldenergyoutlook.org

Agriculture

Fast growing cities will inevitably destroy cropland, which is urgently needed to feed the urban population. This loss has to be compensated in one way or another, creating opportunities in:

- Urban farming
- Intensifying agricultural output of remaining cropland, i.e., by mechanization, irrigation schemes, input of fertilizers and better seeds, educating farmers

Mobility

There is also a need to develop effective public transport systems for a strong growing urban population. In many fast growing African cities, average travel time for all modes of road-based urban transport has increased a lot. Some cities like Lagos, Nairobi, and Luanda are so congested that business people are advised to make only two appointments per day, one in the morning and one in the afternoon. The hours in between are needed for getting from one point to the other. When I was in Lagos last year, I decided to walk by foot from the convention center to my hotel, along one of the main roads. It was considerably faster than by car.

Driven by the FIFA World Cup 2010, South Africa embarked on several mass transport systems to improve mobility. Gauteng Province was one of the most active areas for new transportation projects, including the GAUTRAIN rapid train and the first South African Bus Rapid Transport (BRT) system (in Johannesburg).

When looking for opportunities in this sphere of business, African reality has to be taken into consideration. One time, the City of Douala, Cameroon, made an inquiry for used and new Mercedes buses. I was excited about the possibility of arbitrating a good contract, and asked one of our network experts about the feasibility.

His answer surprised me. The spring system of Mercedes, and other European, buses are generally not aligned for the African reality of heavily overloaded vehicles which is almost a guarantee in Africa.

Buses, which are produced in emerging markets like Brazil, are better suited for needs in other emerging and pioneer markets. Western companies have to learn these types of lessons and adjust their product portfolios, if they want to successfully enter African markets.

The big challenge is to develop business models that can make money. There is a commuter train planned between downtown Harare and the satellite city of Chitungwiza, south of Zimbabwe's capital city. Whoever builds this train system will find it difficult to make money because the local population cannot afford to pay fares that will cover the costs much less make a profit. However, an idea might be to build a "business" corridor ecosystem along the train route and make money from shops and business real estate.

Protection of the Environment

This open sewage canal in Bamako, Mali flows directly into the Niger River without any sewage treatment. (Photo by: Hartmut Sieper)

Many African cities use open canals for sewage transport; and no sewage treatment is in place. This creates various business opportunities in the sectors:

- Water sewage plants and systems
- Waste removal systems
- Waste incineration plants

However, financing is the key bottleneck, as many cities and municipalities have no money and depend on foreign development aid.

Impact of Urbanization on Construction

As indicated before, the construction sector is a key business and investment opportunity. New city dwellers need appropriate housing facilities, according to their financial power. Upper, middle, and lower class residential houses are in high demand in almost all African cities. In Angola alone, one million houses are needed - this for a country with a total population of only 13 million people.

The Angolan government is actively pursuing a gigantic house building program and is looking for construction companies and experienced real estate developers that can handle complex operations and deliver several thousand units at the same time. Lack of financing is the biggest problem in this sphere of business along with high levels of corruption. However, there are ways to navigate these environments as well. For example, the U.S. has a bilateral agreement with Angola covering trade and investment, which offers certain levels of support and protection for U.S. companies. [28]

Of all the subsectors in residential housing, low-cost housing is the most challenging because of high-volume, low-margin operations. However, the rewards can be very high.

The environment of the construction sector in Africa is very different from the situation in the U.S. and many European countries: there is no oversupply, no real estate price bubbles, and definitely not a decrease in

---

[28] For U.S. citizens, contact the U.S. Commercial Services and check out the market research reports at http://www.export.gov.

demand. Instead, there is enough to do for thousands of companies over several decades. It's incredible, but it's true.

It has to be mentioned that large areas of urban settlements are informal. The majority of urban residents in Sub-Saharan cities are living in slums. Some years ago, Brazil introduced a good method of unlocking value in informal settlements. They just formalized these settlements and gave title deeds to the tenants, which enabled them to get mortgage loans. This might be a good blueprint for Africa as well, at least for those countries that allow private ownership of property.

We have to remember that while the forecast for Africa is bright, there is a risk that it might be different. As long as economic growth is outpaced by demographic growth, income per capita will decrease, which will lead to more poverty. Reaching the millennium goal of poverty alleviation is only possible when economic growth is superior. This is the major reason why high economic growth over a long period of time is an essential prerequisite for sustainable development in Africa. Good governance, business-friendly reforms, a reliable financial and fiscal environment, and political stability are needed to initiate, support, and sustain this process. And as indicated in *Chapter 1 – Introduction: The New Africa*, many African countries have demonstrated good progress in these areas for the last 15 years or so.

Conclusion

The population boom in Africa will continue to drive urbanization in Africa. Young people will seek opportunities in the cities.

This explosion in urban population is a serious challenge to urban planning and sustainability. In the case of Johannesburg, it wasn't that the city did not have plans for growth, but the rapid growth of informal settlements, as people came looking for work and opportunities, was overwhelming. In an area allotted in planning for one family, you might find four.

For the entrepreneur on the other hand, urbanization is a bonus in many ways. First, you have a large consumer market in a densely populated area, which can provide lower costs of delivery to customers compared to other areas. Second, there are opportunities in solving the problems faced by rapid urbanization. Third, there are diverse sector opportunities in hubs of economic activity from retail to transport to education to communication.

From a strategic perspective, key urban centers can be used as market entry points because of the microcosm of the national economy located within them. As urban centers spread, firms can follow the natural flow of economic activity to extend their markets. And finally, key urban centers within a region can be chained together to establish a regional presence.

6

Agriculture

Nissi Ekpott

Agriculture in Africa offers many diverse opportunities. This is one area where Africa can have a competitive advantage over every other continent for some of the following basic reasons:

- Agriculture is ingrained in the culture; over 60% of Africans are already involved in farming, though largely subsistence.
- There is an abundance of arable land estimated at a potential of over 300 million hectares, according to the Food Agriculture Organization (FAO).
- The climate is largely favorable.
- There is access to water.
- Africa can meet diverse agricultural requirements.
- There is a market right in Africa - local consumption currently far outstrips production.
- There are relatively low labor costs.

Potential Arable Land and Market Size

Citing an FAO study, the UNEP/GRID Arendal website says that there is a potential of 300 million hectares of rain-fed arable land above current availability.[29] This would be a potential increase anywhere from 150% to 750%. The greatest potential is in Southern Africa. (See graph on next page.)

---

[29] UNEP/GRID-Arendal. Current and Potential Arable Land Use in Africa. *UNEP/GRID-Arendal Maps and Graphics Library.* Accessed online at http://maps.grida.no/go/graphic/current_and_potential_arable_land_use_in_africa (January 11, 2011).

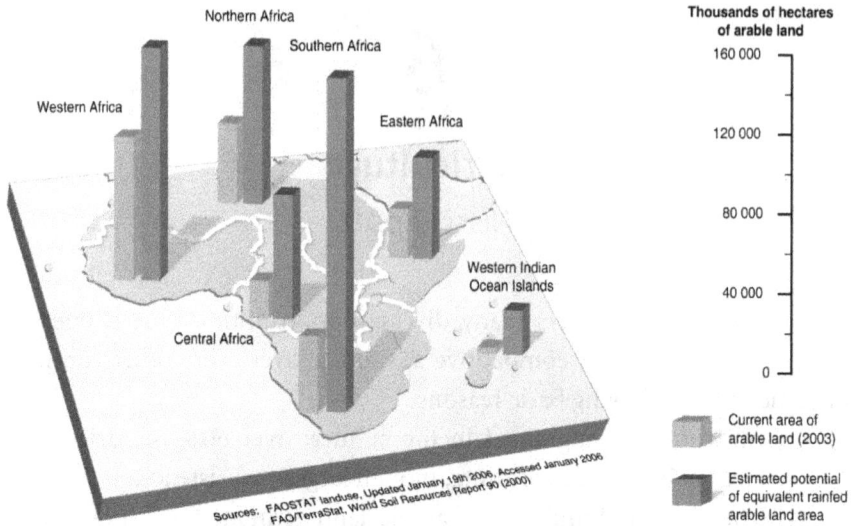

Source: Hugo Ahlenius, UNEP/GRID-Arendal

McKinsey estimates that Africa's agricultural sector currently generates crops valued at $280 billion each year.[30] It believes this could grow to $500 billion in 2020 and as much as $880 billion in 2030.

The vast market opportunities come first from meeting the needs of the large, local population. Many African nations are currently net importers of food, spending billions of dollars on food imports yearly. For instance, the FAO reports that Nigeria imported $2.5-$2.7 billion in agricultural products between 2005 and 2007. Much of this food requirement can be produced locally.[31]

---

[30] McKinsey Global Institute. (2010). Lions on the Move: The Progress and Potential of African Economies. Accessed online at http://www.mckinsey.com/mgi/publications/progress_and_potential_of_african_ec onomies/pdfs/MGI_african_economies_full_report.pdf (January 11, 2011).

[31] Food and Agriculture Organization. (2009). *FAO Statistical Yearbook 2009*. Accessed online at http://www.fao.org/economic/ess/publications- studies/statistical-yearbook/fao-statistical-yearbook-2009/en (January 11, 2011).

Exports and Foreign Involvement in African Farmland

The FAO estimates that Africa's total agricultural exports reached a little over 25 billion in 2007.[32] According to the OECD Development Centre, "The agricultural export composition has experienced a major shift. It has diversified from bulk commodities to horticultural products and, to a smaller extent, processed products...."[33] However, Africa accounted for less than 3% of agricultural exports globally.

But think about it, this is a huge opportunity. Food consumption is expected to rise globally and Africa holds about 60% of the world's unused arable land.

In fact, the focus on African agriculture has accelerated tremendously in the past few years, following the trend where foreign governments, international agribusinesses, investment banks, hedge funds, commodity traders, sovereign wealth funds, as well as pension funds, foundations, and individuals are investing in Africa's land for the purpose of producing food for export.

This is probably by far the biggest single trend involving African agriculture in recent times. Rich nations currently hold millions of hectares of African farmland in a bid to tackle food shortages.

One example is Saudi Star in Ethiopia as reported in The Guardian.[34] Saudi Star has huge facilities, which pack 50 tons of food a day for export to markets in the Middle East. It currently employs over 1,000 women.

Though the benefits of this trend to Africans are still being debated in many quarters, the foreign interest is contributing to an increase in the value of agriculture on the continent. Analysts from Neuafrika.com believe

---

[32] This figure does not include Djibouti, which did not appear in the FAO Statistical Yearbook 2009 data.

[33] Development Centre of the OECD. (2008). Business for Development 2008: Promoting Commercial Agriculture in Africa.

[34] Vidal, S. (March 7, 2010). How Food and Water are Driving a 21st-CenturyAfrican Land Grab. *The Guardian*. Accessed online at http://www.guardian.co.uk/environment/2010/mar/07/food-water-africa-land-grab. (February 10, 2011).

that if this foreign supply is well balanced with local supply, it will add to creating an even larger potential market for agricultural products. Also, if properly handled, it will continue to bring in investment funds, technology, and create jobs. If poorly handled, it has the potential to become another form of colonization.

Land "Gold" Rush

Susan Payne, Chief Executive Officer of Emergent Asset Management, believes that farmland in Africa is giving a 25% return for investors while inviting billions of dollars in foreign investments.[35] It is also believed that these investments serve to uplift and provide jobs for locals.

Ethiopia is not the only African country involved in the land "rush". This land rush was triggered by the worldwide food shortages. The food shortages followed the sharp rise in the price of crude oil in 2008, increasing shortage of water, and new EU policies which stipulate that by the year 2015, 10% of all transport fuel must come from plant-based biofuels.

The first megadeal was announced in 2008 when the South Korean company, Daewoo Logistics, wanted to acquire 2.5 million hectares, equal to one half of the entire arable land of Madagascar. However, the deal was canceled by the new government of Madagascar after the coup of 2009. Some other foreign land deals include:

- Indian companies, backed by government loans, have bought or leased hundreds of thousands of hectares in Ethiopia, Kenya, Madagascar, Senegal, and Mozambique. They are growing rice, sugar cane, maize, and lentils to feed their domestic market.
- In Sudan, South Korean companies recently bought 700,000 hectares in northern Sudan for wheat cultivation; the United Arab Emirates acquired 750,000 hectares; and Saudi Arabia has a 42,000-hectare deal in the Nile province.
- European biofuel companies have acquired, or requested, about 3.9 million hectares of land in Africa.

---

[35] Ibid.

- Saudi Arabia earmarked $5 billion to provide loans at preferential rates to Saudi companies, which want to invest in countries with strong agricultural potential.

Foreigners are not alone in taking advantage of Africa's agricultural potential. South African farmers secured 500,000 hectares of land in the Republic of Congo (Brazzaville) to farm for both export and local consumption. These farmers are following the global trend of securing land in Africa, but being Africans themselves have a heart for the continent. In another example, displaced Zimbabwean farmers were absorbed by the Nigerian government and allocated huge amounts of land. These farmers are said to have turned around the face of agriculture and boosted food production in Nigeria.

Biofuels

Biofuels offer another potential agricultural opportunity. Demand is increasing. For example, the European Union had a policy target that 18 metric tons of biofuels should be used by the transport sector by 2010, when in 2006 use was only 2 metric tons.

Currently, many people argue against the use of edible foods for the production of biofuels as this drives up the cost of food. However, researchers are discovering new plants, such as the Jatropha tree, which is able to produce biofuels in significant quantity yet is not an edible food.

Jatropha is already successfully being grown in large quantities in India, and is used to power trains. An added advantage is the ability of this plant to grow in arid areas and wastelands.

Africa has large swathes of desert areas and wastelands. This is a waiting investment opportunity. It also offers positive environmental impact as these trees would help to stem desert encroachment.

Jatropha can also be planted on other arable land and while the trees are growing this land can be used for the growing of food crops. Jatropha trees, in this case, provide shade for other crops.

Environmentalists favor mixed farming like this against monocultures. On the other hand, research and development regarding fertilizers, plant diseases, appropriate biocides, and the best way to grow Jatropha is still in the early stages.

Palm Oil

In another example, China signed a contract with the DRC to produce palm oil for biofuels on 2.8 million hectares of land. The global demand for palm oil is expected to rise and double by 2020, according to TransGraph Consulting.

The demand for palm oil is not just for biofuels, but for cooking oil and other applications. China is currently one of the largest potential consumer markets for palm oil exports from Africa since palm oil is not produced in China. China has the world's largest consumer market at this time and they have a growing number of preferential trade agreements with African countries. If a foreign investor develops palm oil plantations and processing facilities in Africa along with local partners, he or she can also find favorable paths to export to other high demand markets like China.

While Asia is the key market for palm oil, the consumption of palm oil in the U.S. is also rising. The FDA requirement for companies to list partially hydrogenated oils on labels is driving companies to find alternatives, which includes palm oil.

Palms grow in abundance in West and Central Africa. In fact, the palms grown in Malaysia originated in West Africa. Because palms grow in abundance, they are used for cooking oil and other applications in local markets, so palms are a natural asset to leverage for production, local sales, and exports.

Palm oil is becoming big business in Africa with companies like Sime Darby, one of the largest crude palm oil producers in the world, establishing plantations in Africa. Malaysia-based Sime Darby signed an agreement with the Liberian government to cultivate 220,000 hectares for palm and rubber in 2010.

As mentioned before, there are concerns over how people and the environment will fare as demand increases for palm oil. But some non-profits have shaped strategies to benefit both. All for Africa[36] developed a project called "Palm Out of Poverty," which will benefit both local economies and be environmentally sustainable.

Government Investment in Africa

More African governments are discovering the potential of agriculture and investing in food production as a means to economic development. Agriculture is seen as having a far greater potential to create jobs than any other sector, and thus a means to alleviate poverty.

Through the African Union's New Economic Partnership for African Development (NEPAD) initiative, African governments decided to commit 10% of their national budgets to agriculture. This means good news for investors because more public funding is being channeled into solving the basic shortages in infrastructure, research, and other inputs.

Not only will this increase governmental focus on agricultural productivity, but offers business opportunities to foreign companies to come with technological solutions, which they can sell to government and private sector. At the 2010 African Growth Opportunity Act (AGOA) conference in the United States, that is precisely what the U.S. government promoted to agricultural producers. In addition, U.S. companies through their African partners can export into the U.S. with preferential status through AGOA.

Already, some of these investments have brought about visible solutions and success stories. In Mozambique, for instance, "virtual knowledge centers" are being created to link the country's farm scientists to rural communities and direct researchers to identify problems and create solutions. In another instance, Nigeria, Niger, and Uganda have brought together research institutes, extension agents, and farmers' organizations to introduce improved crop varieties of staples.

In Uganda, farmers are growing NERICA rice varieties in upland areas that had never produced rice before. Uganda is now a net exporter of rice.

---

[36] http://www.allforafrica.org

Malawi is another success story after significant government investment in agriculture. Its success story stunned donors. In 2005, the nation's leadership, tired of going to beg for foreign aid, found ways to empower local farmers through the launching of a fertilizer subsidy project. This subsidy reduced a 50 kilogram bag of fertilizer from about $27 to $6.50. As a result, maize production jumped from 1.2 million metric tons in 2005 to 2.7 million metric tons in 2006 and 3.4 million metric tons in 2007, creating a surplus of 1.5 million metric tons.

The better harvest did not just benefit Malawi, but also neighboring countries. According to the USAID-funded Famine Early Warning System Network, Malawi officially exported 286,589 tons of maize to Zimbabwe by the end of December 2007. Also, the World Food Programme (WFP) sent 32,363 tons of Malawian maize to Zimbabwe, bringing total official exports from Malawi to Zimbabwe to 321,406 tons that year.

Not only did this success make Malawian farmers, including many small scale farmers, better off, it went a long way to prove the potential of agriculture on the continent.

Tackling Challenges of Agriculture While Creating Opportunities

Some of the challenges faced by the agricultural sector in Africa are inadequate infrastructure, e.g., roads, electricity, shortage of inputs like seeds and fertilizer, limited access to equipment and machinery for large scale farming, and land ownership issues. Every one of these challenges offers an investment opportunity.

In the Naivasha district of Kenya, for instance, the challenge of bad road infrastructure adversely affected rose growers. Competing growers got together and fixed up their roads, thereby supporting the industry.[37] The horticulture industry is Kenya's top foreign exchange earner, making $922

---

[37] Vos Iz Neias. (April 20, 2010). Nairobi, Kenya – Effect of Volcanic Ash: 10 Million Roses Ruined. Accessed online at http://www.vosizneias.com/53650/2010/04/20/nairobi-kenya-effect-of-volcanic-ash-10-million-roses-ruined (January 11, 2011).

million in 2009. Kenya exports 1,000 tons of produce and flowers, including roses, carnations, and lilies, per day. This sub-sector employs 50,000-70,000 people directly and over 1.5 million people indirectly.

Another solution, which is systematic, is agriculture growth corridors. They are development corridors focused on the entire agricultural value chain from growing to harvesting to transporting to exporting. They are seen as a means to catalyze both agricultural and economic development. They follow the development of existing transport corridors, e.g., Harare-Mutare-Beira.

In Africa, private sector, government, and NGOs collaborate on such initiatives. Yara International, one of the biggest fertilizer producers globally, and the African Green Revolution Forum (AGRF) are spearheading two agricultural growth corridors – Beira covering Mozambique, Malawi, and Zimbabwe, and Southern covering Tanzania, Malawi, Zambia, and the DRC.

NEPAD has thrown its support into the concept of leveraging the improvements expected along 12 development corridors in Africa for agriculture. They have set up a separate organization called TransFarm Africa (TFA) to spearhead the initiative. Among its initiatives is an enterprise investment fund for agriculture called TFA Transformation Fund.

As these develop, expect opportunities to grow like along transport corridors connecting major cities along the coast and in the interior of Africa. If foreign investors, or businesses, partner with local African agricultural firms, they will be able to leverage more of the benefits from these initiatives.

With Africa's natural assets conducive to agriculture and the increasing demand for food globally, Africa is headed down the path of being the key breadbasket for the world, if developed correctly. This offers extraordinary opportunities for businesses and investors for a long time.

Conclusion

Food is a basic element for human survival, so it is a sector that doesn't require much imagination as to its potential. The opportunities multiply as the global population is expected to be one-third more in 2050 than today. The FAO anticipates that there will be a 70% increase in food demand in 2050 based on the growing global population, but also the fact that people will have moved up the socioeconomic scale and increased consumption.[38]

As indicated in this chapter, Africa is a logical place for pursuing agricultural ventures because of the potential arable land and water. The challenges, such as yields, inputs, and infrastructure, can be addressed with systematic interventions as described here.

The rationale for Africa being a strategic location for the global agricultural food chain is strengthened by the current onslaught of foreign firms leasing land from African nations for agricultural production. It is also strategic in that firms can develop ventures to meet local consumption while exporting to other regions, offering many markets for food products. And markets like the United States provide preferential import mechanisms for certain agricultural products from Africa.

---

[38] FAO. (2009). How to Feed the World in 2050. Accessed online at http://www.fao.org/fileadmin/templates/wsfs/docs/expert_paper/How_to_Feed_the_World_in_2050.pdf (January 21, 2011).

7

Information Communication Technologies
Lauri Elliott

The last decade saw a tremendous boom in ICT in Africa. The key sector is mobile, which continues to grow at astronomical rates. From virtually no mobile phone users in 1999, mobile phone users in Africa will reach 500 million soon. Africa may have double the number of mobile phone users than in the United States within a few years.

In fact, according to the International Telecommunications Union (ITU)[39], Africa is the fastest growing mobile market. In 2010, ITU said that Africa's mobile user growth rate has exceeded 60% annually for the five previous years, double the global average. Africa is, in fact, the first continent where mobile subscribers outstrip fixed-line users.

This is an example how Africa has and can leapfrog the slow development cycle. The story behind the mobile market is that the fixed-line market was controlled by state-owned enterprises, which were inefficient and slow to develop infrastructure. Service was also expensive because of a lack of competition.

Companies like Vodacom in South Africa sought mobile licenses instead since state-owned institutions did not operate in this realm. In addition, it was much quicker to deploy mobile phone infrastructure. And, the mobile phone operators found solutions, such as prepaid services and SMS, so that most people, from poor to rich, could access and use mobile phones.

In the mobile space, Africa leads Western markets with innovative solutions like SMS-based applications and prepaid services. For example, Ushahidi is a web/SMS integrated solution which allows anyone to report

---

[39] http://www.itu.int

critical incident information. It evolved from a request by Ory Okolloh, a Kenyan blogger and former corporate affairs officer for Enablis in South Africa, for any developer who could help her develop a platform so that people could report on incidents in the violence following the Kenyan 2007 elections. The application was developed within a few days. It was also used to report Haiti relief efforts by disaster agencies and track issues and tips in the snow storm coined "Snowmageddon" in Washington, DC in 2010.

Mobile payments and banking have taken off in Kenya with M-Pesa and M-Kesho. Out of a population of close to 40 million, estimates are that 38% of adult users have M-PESA accounts and that over 7.7 million accounts had been registered as of August 2009, according to the report, *The Economics of M-Pesa.*[40]

High-Speed Broadband Boom

Broadband is estimated to contribute 1.3% to economic growth for every 10% jump in availability, according to the World Bank. Unfortunately, this is one area that Africa continued to lag behind Western countries. Only a few years ago, Africa as a whole had less than one terabit/second capacity. This is dramatically changing with the continent's connection to international bandwidth expected to reach over 20 terabits/second within the next few years. The image on the following page shows the major fiber connections, including projections through 2012.

---

40 Jack, W., & Suri, T. (2010). The Economics of M-Pesa. Accessed online at http://www.mit.edu/~tavneet/M-PESA.pdf (January 6, 2011).

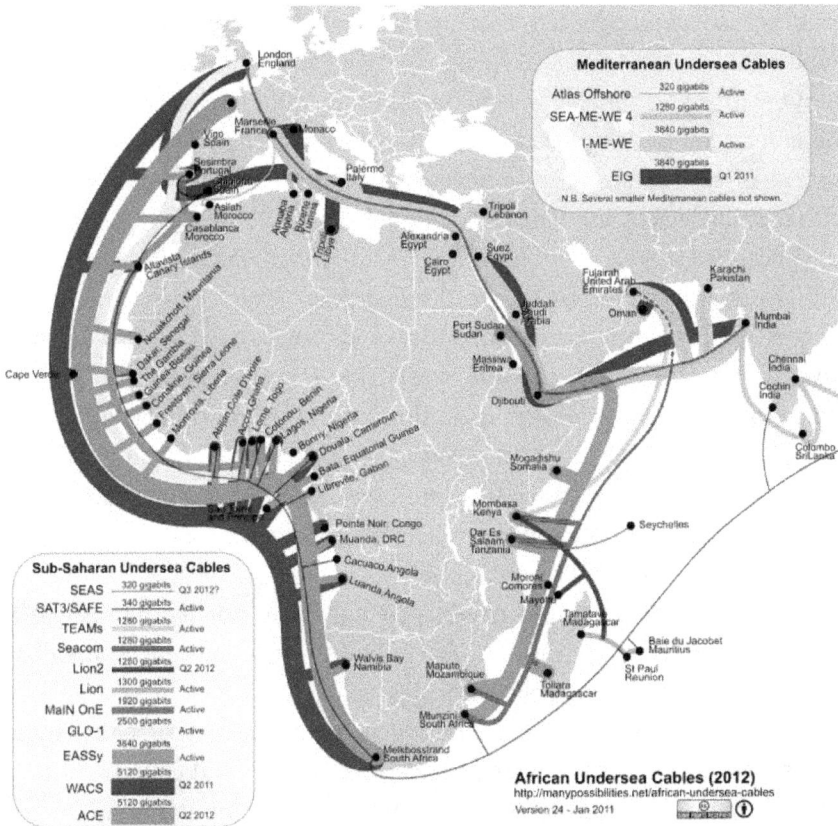

Mediterranean Undersea Cables

Atlas Offshore	320 gigabits	Active
SEA-ME-WE 4	1280 gigabits	Active
I-ME-WE	3840 gigabits	Active
EIG	3840 gigabits	Q1 2011

N.B. Several smaller Mediterranean cables not shown.

Sub-Saharan Undersea Cables

SEAS	320 gigabits	Q3 2012?
SAT3/SAFE	340 gigabits	Active
TEAMs	1280 gigabits	Active
Seacom	1280 gigabits	Active
Lion2	1280 gigabits	Q2 2012
Lion	1300 gigabits	Active
MaIN OnE	1920 gigabits	Active
GLO-1	2500 gigabits	Active
EASSy	3840 gigabits	Active
WACS	5120 gigabits	Q2 2011
ACE	5120 gigabits	Q2 2012

African Undersea Cables (2012)
http://manypossibilities.net/african-undersea-cables
Version 24 - Jan 2011

Source: Manypossibilities.net

Countries along the coast of Africa, where the cables land, get the most immediate benefit due to their proximity. Kenya is a prime example. Kenya's ICT sector was actually waiting like a racehorse in the starting gate for the cable to land and be switched on.

One priority sub-sector in Kenya that benefits greatly from the new bandwidth is business process outsourcing (BPO). Beyond the fact that labor is cheaper, Kenyans speak English well and are better educated in general than other regions of Sub-Saharan Africa. So, Kenya can likely establish competitive advantage in this space, but they were losing their advantage because the cost of ICT infrastructure was three to four times their competitors. When SEACOM landed in 2009, costs dropped and

Internet use climbed even though it is still low compared to Western standards.

One differing variable in broadband users in the West and Africa is that the uptake on the Internet is expected to be primarily from mobile devices instead of computers because of cost and the broad population's comfort with mobile devices compared to computers.

There are still two key challenges for the broadband market – backhaul and access. Backhaul is the land-based fiber optic cable lines. Major countries, such as Nigeria, South Africa, and Kenya, have worked on this to cover at least the major markets in the country. East Africa did well as a region by connecting major areas throughout each country in the East Africa Community – Burundi, Kenya, Rwanda, Tanzania, and Uganda – and between each country, so the foundation to connect a common market of over 140 million people is there. There is progress with backhaul all over Africa.[41]

As an alternative, and to cover areas not easily reached by fiber, is the O3B Networks satellite solution, which will provide affordable broadband anywhere in Africa. They will be fully live in 2012.

The third leg of broadband infrastructure, and the toughest challenge, is access. This is where people are provided the services and equipment to use the Internet. The number of people with both computers and Internet access in Africa is extremely low. In 2008, there were only four African countries in which close to or over 10% of the households had both a computer and Internet access. Two of the countries are in North Africa and the other two are island nations in Southern Africa. (See the table on the following page.)

---

[41] Visit http://www.afribiz.net/insightareas/information-communication-technologies for more details.

Country	Has Computer	Has Internet Access
Mauritius	19.1%	20.2%
Morocco	10.0%	13.7%
Seychelles	10.0%	13.0%
Egypt	9.5%	12.9%

Source: International Telecommunications Union (ITU)

Governments, non-profits, and the private sector are working to provide access in community labs, Internet cafes, schools, and even mobile labs to rural areas. My (Lauri's) company was a subcontractor at one point on a project, which placed a computer lab with Internet access in over 2,000 schools in Gauteng province, South Africa. While the project had a lot of challenges and changes in regime, it finally got the infrastructure in place in 2010 after over five years since its original inception.

When I visited Egypt in 2004, I was excited to see that they had ADSL technology to connect to the Internet at decent speeds, but this was not a typical scenario for the rest of Africa. Some other countries like South Africa introduced ADSL. However, this technology is based on copper wire technology, so it didn't become pervasive because Africa lacked copper wire infrastructure, considering fixed-line infrastructure was, and still is, weak.

Hence, wireless has become the promising channel to deliver broadband to users. Wireless technologies include the external infrastructure, such as metropolitan area networks, and devices, such as mobile phones and data cards. In fact, 4G technology was implemented in South Africa before it was implemented in the United States. This dynamic may change some with external infrastructure as fiber optic backhaul is rolled out.

Opportunities in ICT in Africa

To contextualize the opportunities in ICT in Africa, think of two major occurrences in the United States. First, there was the break-up of AT&T in the mid-80s. Second, there is Internet infrastructure development, which has risen since the 1990s. This is where Africa is headed, just leaving the starting gate.

Opportunities for ICT ventures present themselves in the ICT sector, as well as a supporting sector of other sectors. First, in the ICT sector there are still pockets of opportunities for basic infrastructure, but by and large those opportunities go to very large companies and consortia. However, thinking about the boom of the Internet and telecommunications in the United States, you can imagine the millions of opportunities to provide products and services.

Second, computer and mobile phone equipment and accessories with configurations that will suit the African consumer and at prices they can afford is another opportunity. The college student market in Nigeria is a prime example. This large youth population has disposable income and sees the mobile phone and computer as essentials, according to Nwakego Eyisi, founder of Encompass Analytics of Nigeria, economist, and an Afribiz Media featured columnist.

Nissi, one of the authors, has also found a market for netbooks because of the lower cost and many consumers do not necessarily need the processing power of full laptops in African markets. In markets like Cameroon, netbooks have been popular.

Third, there are still many opportunities for providing training and consulting services, particularly if you are able to work with local partners. But the biggest opportunities, and the fourth area of opportunity, are in developing mobile, SMS, and Internet applications, as well as content, for the local markets.

One of the remaining critical challenges with the school lab project I mentioned earlier is the development of local content. This is echoed throughout Africa. In an interview with Guy Zibi, CEO of AfricaNext Research, he indicated that local content development is indeed a big potential market.

As a sign of the coming growing content market, Limelight Networks, which is a content delivery platform in the United States, partnered with Business Connexion of South Africa. This partnership will provide the platform and content on it to African markets, starting with South Africa, as well as provide African content to the world.

From a segment perspective, expect to find growth in mobile worker and home-based business segments. This will likely take flight in economic hubs, which have strong intellectual and knowledge-based economies, such as South Africa. Lucienne Abrahams and Mark Burke, researchers at the LINKS Center at WITS University in Johannesburg, suggest that the unit of production in South Africa will shift back to the home from the office, or centralized workplaces, and that the government should actually focus resources to support this trend believing they will get better return on investment concerning economic development.

Another segment for ICT is users of smart phones. The market for smart phones is expected to grow by 50% and represents almost one in five handsets sold in Africa in 2011, according to International Data Corporation (IDC).

It is likely that South Africa will represent one of the key smart phone markets as it demonstrated strong growth in 2009 and 2010, even during the economic crisis. But the smart phone market will also grow well in urban, economic hubs like capital cities and regional economic hubs – Kenya, Nigeria, Egypt, and South Africa. You can also look to segments of business like multinationals whose personnel likely possess smart phones for work.

Another way to focus on opportunities is by sector. For instance, travel services over mobiles is a growing sub-sector globally and since the mobile, including smart phone, market is growing well in Africa, it has potential in Africa particularly if you can provide local content.

Another instance is mobile learning. A priority social sector for African countries is education. In most countries, the administration, facilities, and number of professionals needed are lacking to meet demand. Closing the gap is not a short-term effort, it could take several decades. However, mobile phones with broadband to provide access to the Internet can present an entirely different scenario.

And finally, ICT is transforming agriculture in Africa. The Ethiopian Commodities Exchange (ECX) is a world-class, technology-driven exchange making Ethiopian agricultural products available globally. It's amazing this could happen in a country where household ownership of computers and access to the Internet is below 1%.

There are a myriad of innovations and opportunities in Africa for those in the technology sector and those outside of the industry.[42] The key is to focus on those technologies and opportunities that you can understand and use your strengths.

Conclusion

ICT is one of those sectors that provides double opportunities – first as a sector and second as a supporting sector for others. While access to all of Africa will likely take many years, there should be key ICT hubs in each country that businesses can leverage for doing business in Africa within a few years. Typically, these hubs will be economic hubs and large cities.

In recent research by World Wide Worx[43], it was found that business people across the continent were looking forward to the benefits of the landing of the undersea cables. They also found that the majority of respondents were using email, if nothing else, for business communication.

So while it may seem that Africa is disconnected from global business, there is already enough technology and participation which makes it easier and more affordable to manage business in Africa albeit not as broadly as in the West.

---

[42] Ibid.
[43] http://www.worldwideworx.com

8

African Consumer Markets:
An Emerging "Gold" Mine
Nissi Ekpott

Africa's population is estimated at over a billion people, about 17% of the world's population, and is said to be the "youngest" globally. According to United Nations (UN) statistics, 43% of the population is young. Uganda is an extreme example of a young and fertile population. The median age is 15, and the population growth rate amounts to 3.56 % per year (2010 estimate). 6.73 children are born per woman, which is the second highest rate in the world.

Africa's economy measured in GDP per capita is larger than that of India. Also, the income per capita in about 20 countries is higher than that of China. These twenty nations, including South Africa, Botswana, Mauritius, Tunisia, and Ghana, make up a population of between 200 and 300 million Africans, according to Vijay Mahajan, author of *Africa Rising*.

The fact is that African consumers offer more than most people realize, but why do most people not realize what the continent offers? One major reason is because a staggering 400 to 500 million Africans are said to live on less than $2 per day. Much focus in discussion and activism in the past was placed on Africa's poverty, and most media features on Africa focus on this segment of the population which is poor.

Most people got distracted by this and failed to recognize the other 500 million people driving the economy of the continent. The truth is that this richer group has the potential to lift the poorer group out of poverty. One way this will be achieved is by recognizing this potential and investing in it.

Potential investors, especially those who have little experience with Africa, may ask several questions which will be addressed in this chapter:

- How can this consumer base be proven?
- Can consumers be relied on to purchase goods and services?
- Where are consumers found in Africa?
- How best can they be reached?
- Is there potential in consumers in poverty?
- What is the future in African consumer markets?

Can This Consumer Base be Proven?

Mahajan points out that advertisement agencies, economists, and researchers on the continent classify the market into five segments - A to E. Class A and B make up the upper and upper middle class, consisting of 5%-15% of the population, or 50-150 million people. This class consists of people who could be living anywhere in the world. They have access to resources, and are senior executives, foreign expatriates, small business owners, and entrepreneurs.

Class C consists of 35%-45% of the population, or 350-450 million people, mostly blue/white collar workers and self-employed, small-scale entrepreneurs. These people are as ambitious as anyone else in the world, as well as being optimistic, wanting the best for their kids, and believing in the future of the continent.

Combining these three classes, Africa presents a 400-500 million consumer market (with cash flow) that exceeds the United States and the European Union in size but not assets.

Senior fellow Vijaya Ramachandran, at the Center for Global Development (CGD), defines Africa's middle class as those living on more than $5 per day. Above $5 a day would not be enough income to be included in the middle class in the U.S., or other developed countries, but Ramachandran says it is sufficient to be part of Africa's "aspirational class". Ramachandran describes this middle class as having escaped the worst burdens of poverty; able to meet their basic needs in nutrition, health, and housing; not so insecure; and do not risk losing this on a daily basis, which is what it is like for those existing on less than $5 per day.[44]

Going by these estimates, the middle class contributes about $150-$225 billion annually into Africa's economy. This market size should automatically attract any investor in the near and long term.

Another drawing card is the youthfulness of the continent's population. Some researchers refer to them as the Cheetah generation. The Cheetah generation was probably first coined by George Ayittey in his book, *Africa Unchained*[45].

This generation is not bogged down by the baggage of the colonial past - they are ambitious, optimistic, and colorful. For them, the sky is the limit. They are fast gaining access to mobile phones and the Internet. With these new technologies, they are getting to be at par with the rest of the world. Many of them, though having little now, are actively working to be significant economic players and consumers of the near future.

No better example of the potential of African consumer markets, including the Cheetah generation, is the rapid growth of mobile phone users from 54 million in 2003 to close to 350 million in 2008.[46] The number of mobile phone users is fast approaching half a billion. This rapid growth has confounded skeptics who believed the uptake would be poor based on the idea that a consumer base did not exist.

---

[44] Meldrum, A. (May 19, 2010). Africa's Middle Class: Striving to Develop a Continent. *Global Post*. Accessed online at http://www.globalpost.com/dispatch/africa/100514/africa%E2%80%99s-middle-class-striving-develop-continent (January 28, 2011).

[45] Ayittey, G. (2006). *Africa Unchained: The Blueprint for Africa's Future*. New York, NY: Palgrave McMillan.

[46] Smith, D. (October 22, 2009). Africa Calling: Mobile Phone Usage Sees Record Rise After Huge Investment. *The Guardian*. Accessed online at http://www.guardian.co.uk/technology/2009/oct/22/africa-mobile-phones-usage-rise (January 11, 2011).

The Second, or Informal, Economy

The second economy is also referred to as the parallel, underground, or informal economy. These are productive and unproductive activities that are not captured by official statistics. The second economy in Africa is large and vibrant.

Naturally, the true size of this economy is not known because it's a hidden economy, so estimates vary from 30% to as high as 80% of economic activity in different parts of the continent. Many key economic players have remained in this sector to escape the brunt of harsh economic policies, influenced mostly by economic decisions of the past (especially between the 70s and 90s where many of the national economic policies had the effect of crippling business).

The picture has shifted though. From 2000 until recently, some African countries have been on the forefront of economic reforms. Rwanda, for instance, was rated number one globally for improvements in economic reforms in 2010, according to the Doingbusiness.org website.

This increasing rate of reforms offers hope that many of the second economy players will be integrated into the proper economy, able to enjoy the benefits while contributing to the building of these economies. A lot of Africa's consumer market potential lies in being able to harness the wealth within this market.

In South Africa, the community savings scheme of stokvels is worth over 4.8 billion Rand (~$738 million) per year, according to the National Stockvel Association of South Africa (NASASA). Community, or informal, savings schemes exist all over Africa with a focus on preparing for major life events like birth, marriage, and death. As a business person, if you provide a product or service for this segment, you have tapped into a market with ready cash as long as the product or service serves the goal of those saving.

One key ingredient for the success of the mobile telephone companies across the continent was the ability to bridge the economic divide between first and second economies. For example, telephone services were typically offered on a contract basis to customers who were to make payments on a monthly basis. Mobile telephone operators introduced prepaid mobile phone services, which opened the door for the operators into the second economy.

In South Africa, only about 20% of the population could access contract services. The reason being that to obtain a contract, a user needed to meet certain basic documentation requirements. Most users were sidelined. For instance, many of them resided in underdeveloped slums without proper home addresses. The result was that typical users were those from the first, or visible, economy.

With prepaid service programs, anyone with money can now use mobile phones. The result has been rapid growth in mobile phone penetration in South Africa, which is estimated to be over 100%. Many other African countries also have rapidly growing penetration rates, Gabon and Seychelles have also reached 100% penetration. In Uganda, the penetration rate rose from 0.5% in 1995 to 23% in 2008.[47] Only five countries in Africa - Burundi, Djibouti, Eritrea, Ethiopia, and Somalia - have a penetration rate less than 10%.

Robert Neuwirth, in *Shadow Cities*[48], estimates the informal economy in the city of Lagos, Nigeria to contribute about $125 billion to the economy of the nation, and 80% of jobs. This is certainly potential that cannot be brushed aside.

Can Consumers be Relied Upon to Buy?

Mahajan found that African consumers were looking for goods and services just like any other consumer globally. When he did further study, he was surprised to discover that a large number of western and global business corporations were already present and well entrenched in Africa, supplying goods and services.

What was a surprise to Professor Mahajan is a fact every resident on the continent has always known. Africans joke about the reach of Coca-Cola, saying that the drink can be found in every province, region, and rural

---

[47] Ibid.
[48] Neuwirth, R. (2004). *Shadow Cities: A Billion Squatters, A New Urban World*. London: Routledge.

community in Africa. This has been a fact for a long time and applies to several other products and brands.

The key challenge for service providers is how to innovate their products in such a way as to make them affordable for communities of people, whose disposable income is not as large as traditional Western markets.

For instance, Coca-Cola sells its drinks in re-usable bottles. The drinks are sold as "liquid content only". This means that for a buyer to buy a bottle of Coke, he exchanges his empty bottle for a new, unopened bottle. He is buying only the liquid content. This way he does not have to pay for the cost of the bottle. In addition, bottles are small and easier to afford.

Vodacom Congo CEO Alieu Conteh, speaking in the *Africa Open for Business* documentary, says the company did research to discover that the average micro retailer had daily stock of goods valued at $5-$10. This led the company to consider reducing the value of prepaid airtime cards to $2. Immediately after this step, the number of users tripled. The number of users grew from 35,000 in the first week of operation to over 850,000 in its first two years.

Another example is the consumption of Chinese-made consumer items. Consumption has grown exponentially in the past few years, simply because the Chinese have understood this pricing concept. Having come from a country whose poverty rates and economic history share similarities with Africa, Chinese business people have the innate understanding of how to reach and leverage the mass market.

China-Africa trade has grown from $10 billion in the year 2000 to over $100 billion in 2010. A large chunk of this growth has to do with the importation of cheap Chinese products.

In a number of African countries, the Chinese trade model is already moving beyond exporting goods to Africa. Chinese companies are building factories right at the doorsteps of African consumers. They are employing strategies that keep their products affordable, and they are getting the returns.

In Nigeria[49] for instance, UAC, one of the biggest consumer product manufacturers, has spent over $40 million building a water bottling plant. The plant was so large it had to be built 300 kilometers (~186 miles) from Lagos, the bustling commercial capital. However, the distance and initial cost will make its water more costly than that of the Chinese company situated right in the heart of Lagos and which started operations with $300,000. The Chinese company is obviously thriving.

Businesses focused on providing consumer goods and services that meet basic needs at the right prices will have potential for good returns. The consumers are ready to buy because, in many cases, they have no alternatives. There is high demand, but constrained supply.

Mike Koester, a U.S. farmer on a recent visit to Southern Nigeria, its richest oil region, was surprised to discover that there was no source of fresh milk in a region with a population of over 20-30 million people. Such untapped industries abound across Africa.

---

[49] To get a better understanding of Nigerian consumer markets, view the on-demand webinar, "Understanding the Business Opportunities in the Nigerian Consumer Markets," at http://www.afribiz.info/content/understanding-the-business-opportunities-in-the-nigerian-consumer-markets. For other African consumer market information, check out http://www.afribiz.info/insightareas/consumer-markets.

Where are Consumers Found in Africa?

This is a busy intersection in Uyo, Akwa Ibom State in Nigeria. (Photo by: Hartmut Sieper)

A fact, which may surprise the average Western business person, is the African consumer market consists of consumers located in EVERY country of the continent. The typical reports of bad news overshadow and hide the fact that products and services are in demand everywhere, albeit distributed from major hubs.

For instance, Johannesburg, South Africa is fast becoming the "Dubai of Africa", a shopping destination for consumers from the Southern African region of over 200 million people.

These people previously needed to travel to Dubai to shop for some of their needs, including clothing and accessories, cell phones, electronic products, computers, etc. Most of these consumers are themselves resellers within their home communities.

This is a view of Johannesburg Central Business District from Nelson Mandela Bridge. (Photo by: Nissi Ekpott)

Producers and suppliers of these products took up retail space within the Johannesburg Central Business District (CBD), and hence cut out the need for a trip to Dubai. This enabled traders from South Africa and from every other Southern African country easy access to these products.

A trader from, say Malawi, only has to do a road trip to Johannesburg to buy his stock. His travel expenses are significantly lower than having to travel all the way to Dubai. It is estimated that over 400,000 people daily travel the streets of the Johannesburg CBD looking for trade deals, and the numbers are growing. The traders' activities energize demand for other services, such as transport, freight, hotels, food, etc.

Lagos, Nigeria is another hub in West Africa. Traders from the region troop to various major markets in Lagos for their supplies, cutting out the need for them to travel to China and other sources of these goods. And as Africa becomes more urbanized, these business hubs will continue to spur economic activity.

Business strategists realize that though there are pockets of consumers all across the continent, the small scale in some markets is sometimes unattractive. To overcome these challenges, companies are beginning to look at approaching a combination of markets at one time. There are already regional economic communities, e.g., COMESA, SADC, Maghreb Union, and ECOWAS, which offer a basis for developing strategies for trade.

The Market Potential of the Poor

Approximately 500 million Africans are said to live on less than $2 a day. These are said to be poor people. They are those whom the world has learned to pity. Many of them live in slums and in rural areas.

However, there is a fact the casual observer fails to grasp - a dollar in Africa goes further than a dollar in the U.S. This may render the $2/day measure insignificant when considering business opportunities.

Services in Africa are very cheap compared to the West. A haircut in Cameroon costs 50 cents or less. This would be unheard of anywhere in the U.S. Many other services are equally cheap. These Africans, who live below $2 a day, either patronize these cheap services or, in many cases, devise innovative ways to acquire goods and services without exchanging cash. For example, two people might barter to cut each other's hair, or one person exchanges a fish with a person for grain.

Poor consumers innovate to make the most of what they have. Rural dwellers supplement their food needs from small gardens and farms. The market is big on do-it-yourself and home-made solutions, e.g., people fix their broken appliances and build their shanty homes with used sheets or in rural areas with mud.

Community-based solutions can include whole communities collaborating to build homes for each person who needs one. In the rural areas, these are mud homes which require very little maintenance. The amount of money spent on these homes is zero.

Another example is stokvels and thrift societies. These are community banks and lending institutions where participants make contributions at agreed periods and the total contributions are given to each participant in turn until everyone has had a turn. As mentioned before, a study indicated that this informal sector was worth over $4 billion Rand annually in South Africa.

The poor consumer can be characterized with having zero bills. Many do not have monthly bills and they use only what they can afford. If they own phones, they use prepaid airtime. They often will get free education sponsored by the state or development and aid agencies. They live simple lives with minimal needs.

With this type of lifestyle, $2/day becomes a reasonable amount of money and eventually goes into the needs that cannot be provided locally, such as clothes, beverages, improved housing, further education, food, and other basic needs.

In fact, you can find many "luxury" items in African villages where people earning less than $2/day could not normally afford. These luxury items include millions of radios, TVs, lots of Coca-Cola, etc.

If 100 million poor people are able to live on one dollar a day, $100 million is circulating through the economies of the poor daily. In a year, this comes to over $30 billion, quite a significant amount of money.

The challenge facing the investor is how to identify the needs of the poor, and supply these needs at affordable prices. In addition, if the need meeting strategies are able to create jobs for the poor, then the virtuous cycle is in place with the potential to lift whole economies out of poverty and help businesses create and empower their own consumers to increase their buying power.[50]

It is interesting to note that even war-torn communities continue to play economically. There is something about humanity and economics,

---

[50] For further information on developing strategies to create your own consumers in Africa, read the "Creating Your Own Consumers" chapter in *Redefining Business in the New Africa* (http://www.redefining-business-in-the-new-africa.com). You can also listen to interview conduct by Lauri Elliott with Johnny Goldberg, an expert on empowerment in South Africa, at http://www.blogtalkradio.com/afribiz/2010/06/16/creating-your-consumers-in-africa-matching-people-and-profits.

people find ways to be active as long as they have life. A community with no economic activity would only be one that has dead people – the graveyard.

How Do You Find Basic Statistics on Consumer Markets?

It is necessary to note that statistical inefficiencies exist in many parts of Africa. Unlike in developed markets where statistics can be relied on, many African nations have recently emerged from one form of conflict or another, and many of them though in the process of rebuilding social, economic, and administrative systems are still way short of best practices.

Though there's still some way to go, international institutions like the World Bank, International Monetary Fund, African Development Bank, and United Nations agencies have committed vast resources to collect data, as well as strengthen African institutions to improve on data collection. It is this data that enable most economists to safely estimate the size of the market within tolerable error margins.

Any investor planning to get involved in Africa needs to grasp one fact that may sometimes not be obvious – speed. Whenever things begin to change in an African nation, they change rapidly. With the aid of technology, African nations are simply leapfrogging the development cycle. Research and data collection have not been able to keep up.

One of the challenges Africa faces in attracting investment is that before the "golden decade" recognized as 2000-2010, where African economies have experienced greater growth than any other time in modern history, African nations had years of stagnation and negative growth. Investment in research was very minimal, the data usually outdated. In saying this, it's pertinent to note that there are a number of African nations, such as South Africa, whose statistics are of high reliability. From these nations, accurate estimates can be made of the size and characteristics of the consumer markets.

Economic decisions are not necessarily in tandem with current events at the grassroots level because data has not been available. As with any business opportunity and in this case in particular, you will want to do your own market research. You can use channels like the local chambers of commerce, established in every country in Africa.

Future of the African Consumer in the Global Economy

Any keen observer will notice a disturbing, but real trend in the economic architecture of the world today - the average Western consumer has reached a peak, and is most likely to be on a consumption downtrend for a long time until a lot of economic anomalies are corrected.

A look at the world debt trend, in The Economist, indicates that the world's richest nations have taken up the greatest amount of debt.[51] Some economies today have a debt-to-GDP ratio of over 200%. The United States has an overall debt-to-GDP ratio of about 259%.

This indicates that the ability to consume is seriously threatened in the medium and long terms. An economic implosion is a very high probability. If this happens, consumption patterns will change radically and the buying power of the average individual will be seriously diminished. Many economists agree that this is inevitable. The question is when.

What does this mean? Investors and business people need to look at new markets. These new markets will serve to keep Western-owned businesses stable until their nations' economic situations correct. With this in mind, the world is looking at a potential "savior" from economic crises.

Developing economies of Africa, Asia, and South America offer opportunities. Mahajan puts forward an astounding observation - African economies, taken collectively, represent the world's tenth largest economy in terms of GDP! Of course, this needs to be taken in perspective as true economic unity is yet to happen across national borders. However, with the growth of trade blocs, it is only a matter of time until this economic integration happens.

This potentially large economy is sitting largely underdeveloped, requiring vast amounts of investment but possessing enormous potential for high returns. Africa has the capacity to absorb new investments, skills, technology, goods, and services for a long time.

---

[51] Buttonwood. (June 24, 2010). World Debt. *The Economist.* Accessed online at http://www.economist.com/blogs/buttonwood/2010/06/ indebtedness_after_financial_crisis (January 11, 2011).

It also has the potential to become the future breadbasket for the world. Its resources are still largely untapped in a world that is fast running low of resources.

As new industries spring up on the continent, a virtuous cycle is created - workers are employed, new consumers are added, who in turn need new products and services. In this information age, the continent will leapfrog the development cycle.

How Best to Tap the African Consumer Markets

Tapping into the hidden wealth offered by the African consumer markets requires a mindset shift. Large corporations have known this and have been in Africa for decades, right through the darkest of times. Today, opportunities are also opening up for small and medium enterprises.

See beyond Images of Poverty, Conflict, and Corruption

Business decision makers need to see Africa beyond the caricature images of poverty seen on TV. They need to recognize the fundamental changes on the continent, which still has many problems. And, they need to be comfortable with Africa already being on an upward growth trajectory.

Recognize Potential of Growing Youth Population

An investor needs to recognize the potential of a growing youthful population, which offers long-term potential. Then, develop strategies to access this market.

Design Innovative Solutions to Harness Potential of Market

An investor has to design innovative solutions to harness this potential market. The African terrain is very challenging - tough, underdeveloped in many cases, and with multiple issues that could hinder business. Without an above average emphasis on innovation, any African foray is doomed to fail.

South African companies have succeeded in this space; they are involved in over 2,000 projects across the continent. South Africa is among the biggest investors on the continent, if not the biggest.

Alan Knot Craig, former Vodacom CEO, tells the story of deploying mobile phone base stations across rural areas, jungles, war-torn areas, etc. They found ways of being able to overcome the variety of problems in each of the nations.

Innovation should not be limited to product and service offerings only, but has to extend to pricing. It is important to look at ways of making it cheaper.

Craig's story reflects one that is very common across the face of the continent. The level of innovation available at all levels in Africa is simply astounding. You cannot grasp it until you see it.

Know the Market and Develop Appropriate Strategies

Look beyond some of the "impossible" challenges and pictures painted by media. Get on the ground and find out things for yourself. Do your own research. Look for value in the rough diamond. Learn from businesses, which are in Africa already.

You need to be able to reach African consumers at their level, offering them products they can identify with, and gradually guiding them up to what you see as global best standards.

Carry out thorough research of your target market, combining your personal research with information from other sources. Make wise business decisions, limiting risk and boosting impact.

The markets are usually fragmented and underdeveloped, if not undeveloped. Develop a strategy to organize the market. Start from major hubs and work outwards.

Leverage the African Diaspora

Recognize and tap into the hidden strength of the African diaspora. It can bring resources and knowledge to create successful strategies for business in Africa.

Leverage African Culture

Investors should understand and leverage Africa's culture, taking advantage of social, faith-based, professional, and other networks, which are an inherent part of African culture. These cultural networks are one of the most powerful means to furthering any initiative and spreading any message.

Focus on the Long Term

Invest for the long term. Systems in Africa are not efficient in general, but improving. Things take longer than they normally should. This should not be a deterrent. The market takes longer to develop, but a long-term outlook will put an investor in a good place.

Conclusion

The African consumer markets are large and growing rapidly. However, the demographics are much different than Western nations. For example, the consumer markets are very young, fragmented, and have lower income levels than Western markets.

The key to tapping these markets is innovation and shaping strategy to fit the context and consumers. There are several mechanisms for taking advantage of these markets. You can focus your venture in areas with high population density like cities. You can develop a regional strategy to incorporate a larger number of fragmented consumer markets. Another approach is to adapt business models to incorporate both formal and informal markets, as well as address issues of affordability.

There is also a window of opportunity, from now through 2015, during which we see firms having the greatest advantage because the markets have not quite fueled up like in China. There will be a lot of opportunities for decades, but the next five years are particularly good for positioning your firm in the marketplace.

9

Capital Markets

Hartmut Sieper

Another option for creating wealth through Africa is by participating in the African stock markets. In 2010, African stock markets grew 18.7% in local currency, equivalent to about 14.9% in U.S. Dollars.[52] The Johannesburg Stock Exchange (JSE) actually did about 30% in U.S. Dollars due in part to the weakness in the dollar. The Uganda Securities Exchange, Ghana Stock Exchange, and Nairobi Stock Exchange all did well in 2010.

24 African countries[53] are currently involved in stock exchanges – many more than most investors would expect. Of these 24 stock exchanges, about 19 are considered active. However, most of these stock markets are very small. We can divide the existing African stock markets into four groups as illustrated in the tables on the following pages.

---

[52] Data comes from interview with Randolph Oosthuizen of African Alliance Securities. Podcast available from http://www.afribiz.net/content/african-stock-markets-2010-review.

[53] African Alliance Securities (http://www.africanalliance.com) provides both daily and weekly updates on stock market performance across the continent. Africa investor (http://www.africa-investor.com) provides both online and print publications about investing in Africa. Afribiz maintains a category on capital markets at http://www.afribiz.info/insightareas/capital-markets.

Grouping	Exchange	Market Capitalization [54]
Biggest	Johannesburg Stock Exchange (South Africa)	Almost 80 % of the overall market capitalization in Africa of 1 trillion USD is on the Johannesburg Stock Exchange
Minimum 10 billion USD market capitalization and allows institutional investors to buy and sell in reasonable quantities.	Egypt Stock Exchange	67 billion
	Bourse de Casablanca (Morocco)	68 billion
	Nigeria Stock Exchange	57 billion
	Nairobi Stock Exchange (Kenya)	15 billion

---

[54] In U.S. Dollars as of January 31, 2011

Grouping	Exchange	Market Capitalization [55]
Market capitalization between 2 and 10 billion USD	Bourse de Tunis (Tunisia)	9 billion
	Bourse Regionale des Valeurs Mobilieres (Regional stock market includes Senegal, Cote d'Ivoire, Mali, Burkina Faso, Togo, Benin, Niger, and Guinea-Bissau.)	7 billion
	Mauritius Stock Exchange	6 billion
	Ghana Stock Exchange	5 billion
	Botswana Stock Exchange	4 billion
	Zimbabwe Stock Exchange	4 billion
	Lusaka Stock Exchange (Zambia)	3 billion
	Khartoum Stock Exchange (Sudan)	(Not available)

---

[55] Ibid.

Grouping	Exchange
Tiny stock markets with a market capitalization of less than 2 billion USD and characterized by low or very low liquidity and a small number of sporadically traded stocks	Algeria, Cameroon, Cape Verde, Malawi, Mozambique, Rwanda, Swaziland, Tanzania, and Uganda.

The following map is another way to view the development level of African stock exchanges.

African Countries with Capital Markets

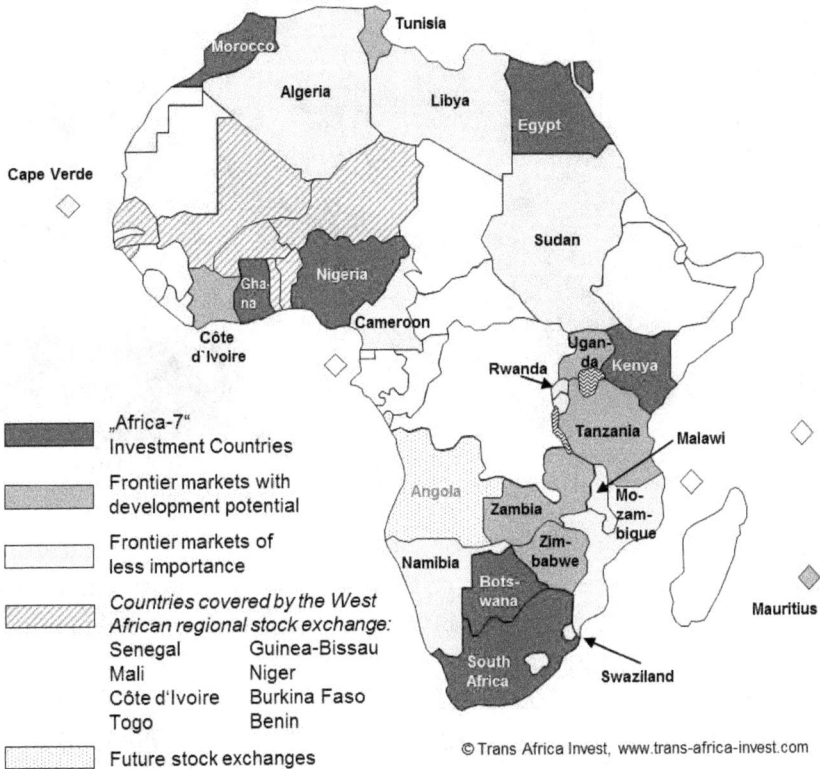

© Trans Africa Invest, www.trans-africa-invest.com

Stock Market Current Developments

On the Zimbabwean Stock Exchange, stock trading is still organized as an open outcry system. However, electronic trading is envisaged. (Photo by: Hartmut Sieper)

Although the Bolsa de Valores de Angola, the Angolan Stock Exchange, has already been legally founded, there is no trading yet and recent reports indicate it will not start trading in 2011. Market watchers estimate that trading will start with government bonds, while stock corporations will be introduced later. One of the major obstacles is the fact that big Angolan companies are very well capitalized; they just do not have the need to go public.

Trading in the first Rwandan counter (Bralirwa) commenced late 2010 in the newly established stock exchange in Rwanda. One Kenyan counter is already dual-listed in Kigali. Furthermore, a new stock exchange has been recently established in Libya.

Not only will new stock markets be launched, there are also considerations to merge existing markets. There are plans to integrate the West African stock exchanges into one big market, as well as the East African Community (EAC) stock markets. Also, to improve liquidity in the regional stock exchanges they are establishing electronic trading platforms. India is partnering with the African Union to develop a Pan-African electronic trading platform.

Regionalization of the stock exchanges is in line with the trend towards regional currencies. Nigeria, Ghana, Liberia, and Sierra Leone are considering creating a new regional currency, the ECO. At a later stage, the ECO could be merged with the West African CFA Franc, which is currently pegged to the Euro. Similar plans are under discussion in the EAC and the Southern Africa Development Community (SADC).

Investment Vehicle Options for Individual Investors

Africa presents an additional option for global investors – those looking to diversify an existing portfolio or to start a new one. There are actually several different vehicle options available to investors outside of the African continent.

Africa Plays

First, you can buy stocks of "Africa Plays". Africa Plays are listed companies having most of their business in Africa, yet are listed on Western stock exchanges. Most of them are mining and exploration companies, e.g., Anvil Mining, First Quantum Minerals, and African Barrick Gold, and are listed on stock exchanges in Canada, London, Sydney, and some of them in the U.S. Therefore, resource stock investors find a big variety of African-related companies they can easily invest in without having a brokerage account in Africa. Many Africa Plays have large market capitalizations and are very liquid.

Some South African companies with a Pan-African focus, such as Murray and Roberts, Shoprite, and MTN, can also be understood as Africa Plays in a broader sense. Investors can even look more broadly to companies in their home markets that have significant operations in Africa, as would be the case with Walmart if the purchase of Massmart in South Africa is completed.

American Depository Receipts (ADRs) and Global Depository Receipts (GDRs)

Some African stock corporations have American Depository Receipts (ADR), or Global Depository Receipts (GDR), that are traded on Western stock exchanges. An ADR is a negotiable certificate issued by a U.S. bank representing a specific number of shares of a foreign stock traded on a U.S. stock exchange. A GDR is a negotiable certificate held in the bank of one country representing a specific number of shares of a stock traded on an exchange of another country. ADRs and GDRs can be bought and sold through your brokerage or bank account in the United States, the United Kingdom, Germany, or other Western countries, depending on your bank customer status.

This is the easiest way to invest into single African stocks. However, there are some disadvantages. First of all, the number of available ADRs and GDRs is very limited. Secondly, the liquidity of these receipts is less than that of the original shares, leading to higher spreads and more volatile intra-day movements. The table on the following page provides a small list of ADRs and GDRs available.

Country of Origin	Companies
Egypt	▪ Commercial International Bank ▪ EFG Hermes ▪ Orascom Construction ▪ Orascom Telecom ▪ Suez Cement ▪ Telecom Egypt
Nigeria	▪ Diamond Bank ▪ Guaranty Trust Bank
Kenya	▪ Kakuzi
Malawi	▪ Presscorp
Morocco	▪ Banque Marocaine du Commerce Exterieure

Some counters can be purchased as original shares, traded at Western stock exchanges, i.e., Maroc Telecom (Itissalat al Maghrib, IAM) at Euronext in Paris. Maroc Telecom is the largest listed company in Morocco. Total Gabon, also listed in Paris, is quite an illiquid small cap.

The above mentioned information does not include South African counters. Stocks and ADRs/GDRs of South African companies are traded on many stock exchanges, including London, New York, and Frankfurt. In New York, ADRs of the following South African stocks are traded:

- Anglo American PLC
- AngloGold Ashanti LTD
- BHP Billiton LTD
- DRD Gold LTD
- Gold Fields LTD
- Harmony Gold Mining Company
- Impala Platinum Holdings
- Sappi LTD
- Sasol LTD

Additionally, Western banks and brokerage firms normally offer to buy and sell any financial instrument that is traded on the Johannesburg Stock Exchange.

Africa-Focused Mutual Funds

Investing in managed mutual funds is the best choice for investors who:

- Want to invest a small amount of money. However, it does not allow the investment to be spread over several single investments.
- Want to follow a buy/hold strategy in the long-term.
- Do not have sufficient time to actively manage their portfolios.
- Want to avoid withholding or capital gains taxes. This is especially true for German investors who have to pay a 25% capital gains tax on each stock market transaction in their individual portfolios; however, sales within a mutual fund are exempted from this tax.

Unfortunately, there are limitations for U.S. investors who want to access mutual funds outside of the United States. Most mutual funds that are managed by European banks and financial institutions do not accept U.S. residents as investors due to very strict Securities Exchange Commission (SEC) regulations, and extraordinarily high risk of litigation. They even limit access to their websites from investors in the U.S. and sometimes Canada and the U.K. Eventually, mutual funds will likely be developed as demand for African stocks increases. However, individual investors should consider pooling together resources with others to increase the amount of money they are able to invest, which will then open doors to more investment vehicles. A typical minimum threshold is $100,000.

Exchange Traded Funds (ETFs)

Another possibility is buying securitized derivatives or Exchange Traded Funds (ETFs). While securitized derivatives, which are structured investment vehicles, are very popular in Europe, ETFs are more common in the U.S. An ETF is a fund that tracks an index, but can be traded like a stock. ETFs always bundle together the securities that are in an index.

It has to be mentioned that choosing the right instrument can be very tricky. The Nigeria Index Certificate from ABN Amro (now a part of the

Royal Bank of Scotland) allows exposure to Nigeria in a simple way, but there are two things that potential investors have to know. First, the Nigeria Index Certificate does not include dividends or scrip issues. While direct shareholders of a Nigerian bank get good dividends and can accumulate new shares when issued, the owner of the certificate gets nothing. As high dividend yields and scrip issues are quite common in Nigeria, direct ownership of stocks will allow better performance. Second, the spread is very significant if you buy the certificate outside the trading hours of the Nigerian Stock Exchange. The spread can run as high as 5.8 %.

The following Africa-related ETFs are listed on the U.S. New York Stock Exchange (NYSE)[56].

Exchange Traded Fund	Description
iShares MSCI South Africa Index Fund (Ticker Symbol: EZA)	Seeks to provide investment results generally equivalent to publicly traded securities in the South African equity market, as measured by the MSCI South Africa Index.
Market Vectors Africa Index (Ticker Symbol: AFK)	The Market Vectors Africa Index ETF seeks to replicate the performance of the Dow Jones Africa Titans 50 Index. The fund represents a broad range of sectors and African countries, including exposure to some less traditional frontier markets.
SPDR S&P Emerging Middle East & Africa (Ticker Symbol: GAF)	Seeks to closely match the returns and characteristics of the total return performance of the S&P/Citigroup BMI Middle East & Africa Index.

---

[56] Source: http://etf.stock-encyclopedia.com/category/african-etfs.html

Online Trading

Online trading is an option for retail investors in a few countries. To date, online trading is offered on the Johannesburg Stock Exchange, Egypt Stock Exchange, and Nairobi Stock Exchange.

Conclusion

Africa's capital markets are among the most attractive investment targets in the world of today. While most Western economies are facing huge problems, Africa is developing astoundingly well. There are strong reasons for that.

African growth markets are very different from shrinking economies with high competition, decreasing margins, and oversupply as can be found in industrialized countries. Many business people and investors believe that business risks are much higher in Africa than in Europe or the United States. This is only partly true. Political instabilities, deficits in legal and commercial law, and infrastructural problems are just one side of the coin.

On the other side, investors will find many opportunities in attractive and expanding markets. This is no longer a secret. International investors already are looking at Africa for both its natural and people resources.

10

Small-Scale Mining: A Golden Opportunity
Hartmut Sieper

Most people believe that mining is outside their grasp as an investment, or business, unless they choose to invest in a publicly-traded mining company. However, there is a niche in mining called small-scale, or artisanal, mining which presents tremendous opportunities for those with moderate to large means. The key is based on the availability of alluvial deposits of minerals or metals, meaning that they are at or near the earth's surface making them easier to extract.

In the West, we generally do not see these types of deposits in abundance any more. However, the United States gold rushes in the 1800s were based on the discovery of alluvial deposits, e.g., the Comstock Lode. But these types of deposits still exist in abundance in Africa. In fact, much of the conflict in the eastern part of the Democratic Republic of Congo that we hear about in the news is due, in part, to alluvial deposits of minerals like coltan which can readily be extracted and sold on the black market.

A single definition for small-scale mining is elusive.[57] The United Nations describes small-scale mining based on volume of minerals mined, 50,000 tons of ore per annum for underground mines and 100,000 tons for open pits. SADC, on the other hand, uses a classification system:

- Micro-scale is manual mining with simple tools and no mechanization.

---

[57] United Nations Economic Conference on Africa. (2002). Compendium of Small-Scale Mining Best Practices. Accessed online at http://www.google.com/url?sa=t&source=web&cd=1&sqi=2&ved=0CBMQFjAA&url=http%3A%2F%2Fwww.uneca.org%2Fsdd%2FCompendium%2520on_best_practices_in_%2520smallsacle%2520.pdf&ei=TStVTefsLIeDtwej4M2QDQ&usg=AFQjCNGiJjrf3xzn5hpYuNiMFNgS8oDaNQ (January 31, 2011).

- Manual is well-organized mining operations, which use some mechanization and requires investments between $10,000 and $100,000.
- Industrial small-scale is mining using up-to-date technology and requires an investment between $200,000 and $3 million.

Note that these figures reflect mid-1990s dollar values, but even in today's dollar value investors can enter projects with as little as $100,000 in gold mining. If this threshold is too great for an individual, then several individuals can pool their resources, reducing the investment and spreading the risk.

So, the scale and investment is small enough, but the opportunity is what brings this over the top. Gold prices have been steadily rising since 2004 and in 2010 the price per ounce passed $1,300.00. According to the World Gold Council (WGC), the price of gold rose 29.2% in 2010. Also, WGC expected demand for gold to remain strong in the short-term due to demand for jewelry in Asia, return of industrial demand, and investors adding gold to their portfolios.[58]

As with any of the opportunities we have provided thus far, we cannot give you a detailed analysis in this book on gold, or small-scale, mining, but we can paint a cohesive picture so that you can consider and explore the opportunities if you so choose.

Gold as an Investment

Gold seems to be one of the key investments in the world of today and tomorrow. There are no liabilities of third parties attached to bullion gold while paper money is just a piece of paper with the promise of a central bank written on it.

What kind of promise do we actually trust when we deal with U.S. Dollars? In fact, there is no real promise. On the U.S. Dollar note, it is

---

[58] World Gold Council. (November 17, 2010). Gold Demand Trends: Third Quarter 2010. Accessed online at http://www.gold.org/download/pub_archive/pdf/GDT_Q3_2010.pdf (January 31, 2011).

mentioned "This Note Is Legal Tender For All Debts Public And Private". There is no longer a statement about the right to exchange dollars for gold. Until 1913, U.S. Dollars could be converted into gold coins to the bearer on demand. What a difference! A century ago, most currencies were backed by gold, directly or indirectly. Nowadays, all currencies in the world are pure paper currencies, without tangible assets as backing. In fact, it is against the rules of the International Monetary Fund to back a currency with physical assets.

However, there is an interesting new development in the United States. In some regions, precious metal coins have been circulated. Some politicians want U.S. states to introduce gold and silver coins as legal tender, referring to the U.S. Constitution.

Now take a look at the huge debt of most of our Western economies, many companies, and most private households. Indebted private individuals, legal entities, cities, counties, states, and nations are slaves to the lenders. The lenders are owners of treasury bonds, municipal bonds, and collaterals of debtors. What will happen if the debtors fail to pay interest or even to pay back the debt?

The reality is most indebted Western economies will never pay back their debt. The United States would not be able to do that even if the income tax rate was 100%. The point of no return already passed many years ago as it stands today. Something has to dramatically change for this to be different. Many holders of U.S. Treasury Bonds are aware of this. So what they have is a piece of paper with a promise that most probably will not be fulfilled.

In fact, there has been a sell-off in the Treasury market. The PIMCO Total Return fund, one of the world's largest hedge funds, recently got rid of all its U.S. government-related debt instruments.

The financial system, and all investments of pension funds, insurance companies, mutual funds, etc., is based on interest. Many market participants are feeling increasingly unwell, but they trust on their ability to get out of the endangered financial instruments, if they have to. This is a very dangerous way of thinking. If a horde of elephants wants to trample through a narrow door, there is no way out. So, what options do we have?

Gold represents a value in itself. It is a rare chemical element that cannot be produced out of other elements. It is not connected to any paper currency. There are no liabilities of promises of third parties attached to it. Gold is being traded all over the world.

The possession of bullion gold was forbidden for U.S. citizens from 1934 to 1971. It cannot be ruled out that having or buying gold may become illegal again. From my point of view, this threat is biggest in the U.S., followed by the European Union. Countries like Switzerland, which is not a part of the EU, Dubai, Singapore, Hong Kong, and Panama, are much more secure places.

I don't think that there will be any restrictions on gold ownership and trading. If you are a U.S. citizen, you might consider participating in a gold mining company instead of owning gold. Africa is full of promising opportunities.

Gold'en' Opportunities in Africa

Metals like copper, platinum, and chromium are used in industry and therefore exposed to economic cycles, which might become a problem in a recession or depression of the Western economies. Gold is different. If you understand gold as the ultimate currency, then the basic business model of a gold mining company is virtually producing money. So, it might be a good idea to have ownership in a gold mine somewhere in Africa.

During intense research on that topic, I found out that there is an interesting market niche in small-scale mining in countries like Ghana, Zimbabwe, Tanzania, the DRC, and other countries with alluvial gold deposits. Many of those deposits are small in size but have high grades. They are too small for the big mining companies like AngloGold Ashanti, BHP Billiton, and Rio Tinto; hence there is very little competition. Alluvial deposits along current and ancient rivers are shallow, have thin overburden, and can be mined easily with some low-tech equipment.

You only need a prospecting or mining license, some capital for purchasing the equipment and hiring people, some knowledge about the processes, diesel supply for power generation, and a water source on the ground. Basic equipment includes a bulldozer for earth movements, a stone crusher, a separator, a pump with a water pipe, and maybe a mining shaft. Then, you can start.

Last year, I visited some small-scale mining operations in the Greenstone belt zone of Zimbabwe, where there are a lot of artisanal gold miners. Most of them do not have enough capital for buying machines. They take the ore out of the ground with very basic means and bring the ore to a better equipped gold mine to process it.

A mechanical separator can get approximately 1/2 of the gold out of the stones. For this work, the processing company may keep a small percentage of the gold output, as well as the sludge which still contains a lot of gold. An even better equipped company, which has the possibility of processing the sludge by chemical treatment, will make huge profits by just processing the waste of small-scale miners. Some listed companies like DRG Gold and New Dawn Mining have already successfully started this business in Zimbabwe. But there is room for more.

This is a small-scale gold mine in Zimbabwe, close to Kadoma. (Photo by: Hartmut Sieper)

This opportunity is not out of range for middle-income individuals or groups. There are several successful small-scale mining operations, including gold, that we are aware of and we have formed alliances to expand and replicate the business models around gold mining, specifically designed for entrepreneurs and small investors.

Besides small-scale gold mining, we will scan certain regions to identify additional areas with mineral resources and apply for prospecting licenses. In this respect, a sophisticated new reconnaissance technology for mineral resources is being used.

In order to make a difference from the old business model of exploiting Africa, the project owners will tithe 10% of the net profits and will invest a further 20% into other viable projects locally, especially in agriculture and drinking water supply. By wisely using the natural wealth, it will be possible to uplift people, communities, regions, and countries.

As these projects are for-profit enterprises, development aid is not needed. Projects of this kind require investors, not donors. Only viable, profitable projects can be and should be multiplied.

Conclusion

Gold's benefits include being a rare mineral that cannot be substituted, a tradable asset, and not "fiat" money. There is a wealth of it in Africa.

We only have to imagine the gold rushes in the U.S. West in the 1800s to imagine the potential in Africa, which has more deposits than the U.S. There are assets lying fallow.

The winners in the U.S. gold rushes were those who got in early and found the sources of gold, as well as those who found a niche in the gold industry ecosystem like shipping companies, shovel makers, and minters. Because of the underdevelopment of this sector in Africa, there is still a lot of space for winners in the African gold sector.

Building a New Framework for Business

11

Inclusive Business in Africa

John Luiz[59]
Jonathan Goldberg[60]
Lauri E. Elliott

The principles of good management apply universally and, in this respect, doing business in Africa is much like doing business elsewhere – with some nuances. However, having said that, it is evident that the business environment (including the social, economic, legal, and political dimensions) is highly complex in Africa because of the continent's unique history, diversity, geography, political, and institutional landscape.

The result is that one cannot do business here without recognizing that this legacy has shaped the business environment in ways that cannot be ignored. And, along with the legacy, future trends call for new forms of business that will be profitable but also consider people and the planet.

Realities of Doing Business in Africa
A multinational corporation entering South Africa with the aim of using it as a platform to do business in Africa needs to understand that it will have to confront the country's apartheid legacy and the country's attempt to overcome that legacy. The South African government has adopted a complex system in these efforts that affect various components of the business environment. A case in point is Broad-Based Black Economic Empowerment (BBBEE) legislation, which requires black ownership so as to redistribute assets to those who were previously disadvantaged under

---

[59] http://wits.academia.edu/JohnLuiz
[60] http://www.globalbusiness.co.za/

apartheid. This legislation has been contentious, and certainly experience elsewhere on the continent has not been without controversy or corruption. However, it is clear that political and social stability in South Africa is contingent upon rectifying these injustices.

From an international business perspective, this raises the apparent costs of doing business on the continent and may elicit the question of why businesses should have to pay for crimes of the past. However, what is often overlooked is that it does have unexpected payoffs. Local empowerment companies bring with them local knowledge and contacts, which may be of benefit and allow more effective access to the local market. The South African case is not unique, and various African countries have adopted analogous indigenization programs with similar objectives and specifications.

Also, any company doing business on the continent must take into consideration the complexity of leading in such a diverse context. Managers in Africa need to contend with challenges that may be foreign to outsiders.

There is a sense of social responsibility that goes hand in hand with leadership in Africa. It is impossible to be only profit-driven and be sustainable on this continent with its culture, its challenges, and its history. A manager needs to deal with the scourge of poverty, unemployment, and HIV/AIDS not only because it is the right thing to do but because it makes good business sense in a region where firms are expected to be embedded in the community in which they operate.

Leaders in industrialized countries may deal with diversity at a superficial level at home (e.g., gender, race), but in Africa they are forced to confront diversity in its most stark manifestation where it has often erupted into real conflict. Operating in these surroundings requires a sensitive, and often brave, response from companies. This, in turn, affects the human resources environment in Africa and allows one to understand why the region has developed such complex labor relations systems and why trade unions have taken on their particular roles.

And in terms of strategy, it is necessary to be creative and innovative, as well as understand the peculiarities of this market. For example, there is a strategic challenge facing entrants into Africa about whether their existing products are even saleable or scalable on the continent. A lack of purchasing power, or a lack of infrastructure, in developing countries suggests that "down-scaled" or even different product portfolios might be required to harvest this potential. Thus, a business needs to ensure that its products are affordable, available, accessible, and attractive in the market it is entering.

And if not, an important strategic question arises, "Should a new product that suits the purchasing power of the African market concerned be developed?" And, if it is, will its costs of development be covered by cash flows emerging from the market involved? Also, will the contextual conditions and the operating infrastructure permit scaling of the opportunity?"

However, it is important to understand that starting operations in Africa within the next five years can be a strategic advantage moving forward. If you look to Africa for short-term gains only, you will likely not find success. Just as with emerging regions like Brazil or China, the long-term outlook is strong and more sustainable.

Some good news, as previously mentioned in this book, is that the business atmosphere in Africa has improved dramatically over the past decade and is likely to continue doing so. For example, NEPAD seeks to provide business with a predictable environment in which the rules of the game are understood and more familiar. This will make adaptation easier.

But there are still threats to the process. NEPAD has not received uncontested support both by the general populace, who question its pandering to Western ideas, and by renegade regimes clinging to power.

Bad neighbors also still exist in Africa and contagion from these neighbors remains a threat and, indeed, there is ample literature on the negative externalities which go with bad neighbors, as in the case of the current situation in the Ivory Coast and the spillover of people into Liberia.

And, the consolidation of the political and economic liberalization since the late 1980s has yet to be completed. Therefore, the threat of reversal remains real, but declining.

However, the potentially higher risk in Africa is matched by significantly higher returns and this has seen a recent scramble for quality assets in Africa as companies recognize the potential of these large, untapped markets. Incomes are rising in Africa and soon the large population will translate into significant consumer markets.

Empowering Your Bottom Line by Empowering Others

While South Africa's BBBEE codes have been cause for contention, the revised codes of 2007 introduced a framework that is surprisingly insightful at its foundation. It is actually a framework that would be broadly beneficial to business looking at how to shape successful businesses in Africa, no matter the country.

One of the key problems with the original set of BEE codes is that it focused on achieving equity through ownership schemes primarily. In this context, some blacks became wealthy in South Africa while many others remained behind. And, firms who entered arrangements often did not find mutual value in the arrangement other than they had fulfilled requirements of doing business with the South African government.

There are seven strategies, or categories, within the BBBEE codes, which are social development, procurement, skills development, employment, enterprise development, management, and ownership. If you create a holistic framework, using most, if not all, of the strategies you can build your company's internal capacity and consumer base.

The starting point for being able to empower your bottom line by empowering others is the mindset of the leadership of the enterprise. Without a sustainable commitment to the new approach and cascading it through an enterprise, the initiative is bound not to produce significant results. If the leadership team is not committed to this approach, cannot have a change of mindset, and understand that business cannot carry on into the future on the same basis as before, the results of BBBEE will not be achieved.

BBBEE should rather become part of the strategic imperative of enterprises as the only way to survive and prosper in South Africa. In order to be sustainable it must become truly broad-based and not only benefit a small minority.

On the African continent, many countries have not had a participative empowerment approach and although they have been independent for longer than South Africa, they are still grappling with this problem. The consequential result is draconian legislation, for instance, introduced in Zimbabwe which states that businesses over the next 5 years must have 51% black Zimbabwean shareholding.

Political interference has taken shape in many of these economies as a direct result of not bringing a sufficient number of the population into the main stream of the economy.

The proposed approach is founded on the principle of a broad-based approach as opposed to a narrow one. This is put out in the BBBEE Codes of Good Practice[61] and the approach is for enterprises to score up to 100 points for BBBEE across the seven distinct categories.

The question is how do enterprises get into this more sustainable broad-based approach of transformation? It can be deduced that the approach is far broader than the past practices and should, if correctly implemented, have a far greater impact on transformation. The key to unlock this desired result is, however, implementation.

As a result of the generally poor scores in the element of management and employment equity that make up 30% of the scorecard, pressure is placed on enterprises to score well in the other categories.[62] This correctly modeled could create the opportunity in getting a shift away from the emotional charged issue of ownership requirements. For example, Microsoft has successfully developed a BBBEE strategy, approved by the South African government, which is not based on ownership schemes.

---

[61] Detailed information can be found at the Department of Trade and Industry of South Africa at http://www.dti.gov.za/bee/beecodes.htm.
[62] Goldberg, J., & Balshaw, T. (2008). *Broad-Based Black Economic Empowerment: Final Codes and Scorecard.* Cape Town, South Africa: Human & Roussau Publishers.

The key to BBBEE strategy for most enterprises must lie in the 15 points allocated for skills development. Most South African enterprises currently are facing a major skills shortage in key areas of their enterprises. This will likely be the case for foreign firms as well, and be a typical scenario across Africa.

It is therefore a business imperative to invest heavily in skills development for a sustainable future. This approach calls for a new strategic intent, through skills development, and for an enterprise to buy into implementation of BBBEE based not only on the "right" thing to do but the "best" thing to do for the sustainability of the company. The underlying assumption is that if a business rationale for implementation of an initiative could be found, it has far greater chances of succeeding than a legislative penalization approach.[63]

Moving forward BBBEE schemes can be incorporated into competitive and sustainable strategies, instead of solely legislative requirements, for businesses. While there are costs associated with BBBEE, these costs can be seen as investments for sustainable business practices in South Africa and even applied to other markets in Africa and emerging regions.

A Case Study of BBBEE in South Africa

A motor manufacturer, such as DaimlerChrysler South Africa, could be taken as an example. They will not be fined or penalized directly for not implementing the Act through legislation. They do, however, do business with the Government insofar as the sale of vehicles and trucks are concerned. They further rely heavily on government incentives for their exports programs. It is in this area when the Government deals with them, where they apply the legislation to impose direct pressure on DaimlerChrysler South Africa to comply with BBBEE. Further down the supply chain, a family-owned consultancy firm wanting to do business with DaimlerChrysler South Africa would have to get a good BBBEE score to

---

[63] Ibid.

enable Daimler Chrysler South Africa to get a good score under procurement.

A motor manufacturer is limited in the area of procurement in that major procurement comes from international enterprises that are not in a position to comply with the codes from an ownership perspective. Private imports are excluded from the measurement. This will translate into even more pressure being imposed on those suppliers in order to comply with the legislation and Codes of Good Practice.[64]

The above knock-on effect is illustrated by the consultancy firm now having to get its empowerment credentials up to speed. It would also be forced to look at its own procurement. Here, it could be assumed that one of the major expense items is travel. The consultancy will now put pressure on its travel agent to become BBBEE compliant.

The family-owned travel agent, whose quest, in time, is to have a good broad-based black economic empowerment rating, looks at its suppliers and so on. The cascade effect of BBBEE will be experienced throughout most enterprises' supply chains – any business that ignores it will be ill-advised and this would lead to a loss of business. This is deemed a much better way to monitor implementation than through government monitoring and constant political pressure.

As a result of this knock-on effect, all these enterprises have to focus on the elements of the scorecard. The elements that bring the sustainable benefits to your future customers and employees are procurement (as in the above example), skills development (the only way to ensure the right employees to do the job), enterprise development (creating more Black entrepreneurs to participate in the main stream of the economy) and socio economic development (help by the enterprise linked into aspects of the business like in the General Motors example above). The elements of employment equity and management control are therefore a natural progression underpinned by a strong skills development initiative.

---

[64] Goldberg, J., & Balshaw, T. (2005). *Cracking Broad-Based Black Economic Empowerment.* Cape Town, South Africa: Human & Rousseau Publishers.

Ownership then becomes not a necessity, but a personal enterprise's choice of whether the enterprise needs to go down that route strategically.

The Broader Application of Inclusive Business

From a business perspective, I totally agree with others that handing part of your company over to a group just because of its ethinicity, or disadvantaged status, is not a value proposition. I would refuse and take my business elsewhere. (I [Lauri] am African American so I can say this more directly perhaps than others).

However, if I can create value for my firm while addressing transformation or empowerment requirements, I am all for it. In fact, I systematically look for ways to do so.

One of today's mantras is "Doing Well by Doing Good." This is really the context in which business operates today globally, not just in Africa. We need to be concerned with the triple bottom line - people, profit, and planet. We need to create sustainable societies and economies from which all can benefit. Hence, the term "inclusive" has become a key message for today and the future.

There are innumerable ways to precisely define inclusive, depending on the context. Suffice it to say that when we think of business, or inclusive business, we are speaking of firms trying to engage with low-income consumers and communities for the purpose of sustainable development. Sustainable development typically covers social, economic, or environmental issues.

The concept of inclusive business has not dominated the business environment as of yet, but its profile has significantly risen in the last five years. Multinationals like Cadbury, Coca-Cola, and Unilever have implemented inclusive business models. Whatever the motive for implementing inclusive business models, there is no denying that by developing inclusive business models these companies will ultimately be benefiting their bottom lines, building strong foundations in emerging markets.

The concept of inclusive business models is about to go mainstream, if it hasn't already. The last several decades of exuberate growth, but increasing economic inequity has put social, political, and economic pressure on governments around the world. This pressure, if not released well, will create negative consequences. Business is part of the solution as recognized by the call for inclusive growth from global business leaders at the 2011 World Economic Forum. So, the key question is no longer if or when to do it but how you should do it.

This is where we return to using the principles behind South Africa's BBBEE code as a framework for inclusive business. As discussed, doing business in Africa requires dealing with its legacy and future trends, which means that firms need to find innovative ways to deal with poverty, unemployment, and social issues in the communities in which they operate.

Like strategic philanthropy, I believe that inclusive business models should bring value to the business enterprise. The approach I use most often I call, "Creating Your Own Consumers". In essence, by helping people build sustainable lives both socially and economically, you are developing your consumer base.

Let's explore one scenario. Besides poverty, unemployment, and social issues, companies often have difficulty finding skilled workers in local markets. Let's say a technology firm, ECHOSOUND, which will be providing products and services to retail customers, wants to enter a local African market. How can the company use the seven strategies to its benefit?

First, knowing that an increasing number of skilled workers will be needed to serve the local market in the medium term, ECHOSOUND decides to sponsor a math, science, and technology program for a secondary school serving low-income students. This would be applying the social development strategy aligned with business objectives.

As the students finish successfully and go on to university, ECHOSOUND provides scholarships and internships for students during university. This is applying the skills development strategy.

Once the students complete college, ECHOSOUND hires them, which applies the employment strategy. The additional bonus is that through internships and summer work programs the students not only learned about basic workforce skills and made some money, but also became familiar with ECHOSOUND's company culture and operations. Having designed innumerable entry worker programs and consulted with companies with low-performing, entry-level workers, I know the transition from school to work is costly to a company when it takes a well-paid, skilled worker two to three years to reach adequate performance.

As these former students work for ECHOSOUND for three to five years, they then become assets to the company and potential managers. With this virtuous cycle, ECHOSOUND is developing both the local community and itself. The people ECHOSOUND has brought up through the ranks and possibly made managers, perform well and understand the business.

If some of ECHOSOUND's talented personnel decides to go out on their own (the company should expect this), ECHOSOUND can create enterprise development programs to help these entrepreneurs, if the business ideas fall within the business ecosystem of the company. And, as these entrepreneurial enterprises develop, ECHOSOUND can procure goods and services from them. Therefore, ECHOSOUND implements both the enterprise development and procurement strategies.

The company can also work on an ownership strategy by offering employees shares in the company, and/or elevating senior management to owners in the company. Some companies may choose to follow an employee-owned company model like Southwest Airlines in the United States.

In South Africa, a great example is Axiz, one of the leading technology distributors in South Africa. Axiz was started in the late 1980s by Anthony Fitzhenry and Simon Hodgson. Under Fitzhenry's leadership, Axiz transformed to an employee-owned company in 2003. In addition, they have developed several inclusive business models also working with communities like a tree planting venture.

In this scenario, the methods used by ECHOSOUND are typical programs companies do anyways in the West to some degree. So, the ideas are not totally foreign. However, if implemented aligned with South Africa's BBBEE codes, or other empowerment or transformation requirements in other African countries, companies set great foundations with government and society in African countries with the potential to reap rewards as well.

There are innumerable sources and examples of inclusive business models[65], so one model does not have to fit all. The key is to know your business strategy, then find or create an approach that fits your business imperative.

Transformation, empowerment, and inclusive business are no longer costs of doing business, but investments made to grow a sustainable business. And as these approaches become widespread, they will help directly and indirectly address the broader, larger issues of poverty, unemployment, disenfranchisement, and other social dynamics at play.

Conclusion

The realities Africa faces today are similar to most developing regions, and alarmingly on the increase in the West. There is no easy answer in the complex environment of today's world. Solutions need to be holistic and systematic, focusing on the causes not the effects.

Inclusive business is certainly not a new idea, but its evolution, still in progress, to a mainstream concept is different. In some respects, some businesses have found the cost of doing business that is not inclusive is higher than the cost of doing business that is inclusive. What is clear is that many firms with long-term strategies for emerging markets are shifting priorities and approaches.

In Africa, many governments have some level of transformation requirements, such as minimum indigenous ownership requirements. However, a holistic approach that benefits both the people and business on a large, systematic scale is not evident. The effect is that governments will try to institute more regulations to make sure their people benefit. This, in the end, is not necessarily the best scenario for the people or the business.

---

[65] For further resources on inclusive business, visit
http://www.afribiz.net/insightareas/inclusive-business.

However, inclusive business models will help both governments and businesses meet their imperatives while benefiting people.

12

Discovering Opportunities in African Consumer Markets
Nwakego Eyisi[66]

As you begin to shape strategy, understanding the context of business in Africa, you want to be able to collect broad snapshots about market opportunities. One way of doing that is by using socioeconomic demographic data from reliable sources like the World Bank, African Development Bank, the International Monetary Fund, and African governments. In most cases, you can find data at least five years back to identify trends and up-to-date as of the last fiscal year.

Snapshots help to identify paths to explore, but do not give you enough detail to make informed decisions. You must have a balance of data sources, as well as types of data and a sufficient level of detail to make informed decisions. So, snapshots are appropriate for your initial research and opportunity considerations.

Socioeconomic Data and Insights for Investors

Socioeconomics engages economics to study society while data is factual information used in decision making. Society is made up of individuals often grouped by income, occupation, etc. It could also mean a region or a country. In the context of using socioeconomic data to navigate business opportunities, data actually represents people and how they move or change over time.

---

[66] http://nwakegoeyisi.com/

Through socioeconomic variables like demographics, employment rate, literacy rate, GDP per capita, telephone usage rate, Internet penetration rate, etc., we begin to paint a picture of individual behavior and consumption patterns over time. Because the data occurs over time, it also provides historical insights regarding policy and socioeconomics. This, in turn, arms the investor in answering crucial questions like:

- What drives individual consumption for a particular market?
- What does poor personal computer ownership despite improving incomes mean for consumer markets?
- What do five children to one woman fertility rates mean for consumer markets in the healthcare (hospitals and pharmacies) space?
- What drives rural urban migration and implications for consumer markets and the wider economy?

However, some of the answers to these questions also lie in policy. Understanding both the consumer and the context (business environment and policy) will help investors navigate consumer markets in Africa. The starting point, however, lies in the ability to slice and dice socioeconomic data in a manner that provides insights and opportunities for new markets and business ventures.

For example, if a large country has low Internet usage or low personal computer ownership and per capita incomes have been rising steadily for about ten years, it is probably a sign to investors that the ICT market is ripe for picking. Likewise high birth or fertility rates, inadequate hospitals, insufficient public funding of healthcare, and expensive hospital rates are signals that private sector participation is needed.

Low home ownership rates in a country with steadily rising incomes are a pointer to a potentially rich mortgage market. A large number of people as a percentage of the labor force employed in agriculture, as well as high food prices, means that demand exceeds supply and that significant business opportunities lie in this sector due to a large consumer market.

It is socioeconomic data like in the examples above that contains information about people's habits, economic decisions, welfare, and government policy. And, in a sense, reveals a great deal of information an investor needs to know about opportunities in consumer markets.

Socioeconomic Data and Market Innovation

Socioeconomic data is not only useful for an investor entering a market; it is also useful for expanding and remaining in that market. Cell phone companies are here to stay in Africa, but they also have to find ways to remain relevant and competitive. This is another area where socioeconomic data has been instrumental in pushing innovation.

For instance, mobile phone companies are aggressively investing in mobile banking across Africa as a way of increasing market share and remaining competitive. This is because socioeconomic data has revealed that bank penetration rates in Sub-Saharan Africa are very low. Nigeria, for instance, has 150 million people but only 23 million bank accounts (of which a good number are multiple accounts held by one owner). This is due to a combination of factors like poor infrastructure and irregular income among others. The good news is that people across the continent want to own an account for business, and other reasons, so the market is ripe for picking.

Discovering Opportunities in Fertility Data

Fertility Rate

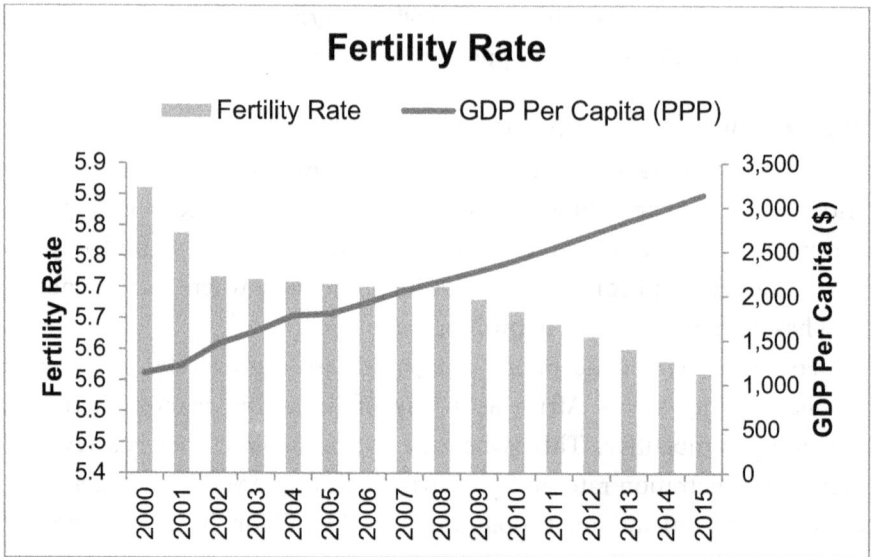

Fertility Rate Compared to GDP per Capita Rate. Source: United Nations/OECD

In this example, the average birth per woman (fertility rate)[67] has gradually declined from six to five currently in Nigeria. This means that the average Nigerian woman will have about five children in her lifetime. Decreasing birth rates is synonymous with a growing economy and this trend is

---

[67] Total fertility rate represents the number of children that would be born to a woman if she were to live to the end of her childbearing years and bear children in accordance with current age-specific fertility rates. Sources: 1) United Nations Population Division. (2009). *World Population Prospects: The 2008 Revision* (advanced Excel tables). New York: United Nations, Department of Economic and Social Affairs. Available at http://esa.un.org/unpd/wpp2008/index.htm, 2) Census reports and other statistical publications from national statistical offices, 3) Eurostat: Demographic Statistics, 4) Secretariat of the Pacific Community: Statistics and Demography Programme, 5) U.S. Census Bureau: International Database, and 6) household surveys conducted by national agencies, Macro International, and the U.S. Centers for Disease Control and Prevention.

expected to continue. Health expenditure as a percent of GDP was only 7% ($8 billion) on average between 2003 and 2007.

The Nigerian population is underserved in this area and there are opportunities for greater private participation in a nation where personal incomes are rising. Moreover, the size of total private expenditure (70%) on healthcare indicates that the market is ripe for further private sector participation.

Insights for Investors

In this example from Nigeria, a large market totaling millions of people and incomes has been increasing steadily since 2000. Government expenditure on healthcare is grossly underweight so that private participation is needed to fill the gap. Government commitment to improving healthcare delivery will lead to policies that would open up this sector to greater private participation. Excess demand over supply will guarantee very good returns and is a signal that there is more room for private investment. Nigeria has experienced healthcare professionals to keep up with new investments. Finally, there are existing private hospitals that have been successful in providing healthcare service so that new investors have a model to follow.

This data suggests huge opportunities in the healthcare space for women and children. Significant investment is required in pediatrics, obstetrics and gynecology, maternity wards, etc., to plug the supply gap. Already 70% of total healthcare expenditure by individuals and households goes to the private sector. This sector will provide good returns to investors since a large market already exists.

Also, high prices for health services are a signal that more private sector participation is needed and a guarantee of higher returns for investors. As more producers move in, it will create incentives for innovation in the healthcare devices and technology market, etc. Furthermore, a growing economy, where incomes are rising, is more than adequate ammunition to drive investment in this sector.

Discovering Opportunities in GDP Per Capita Data

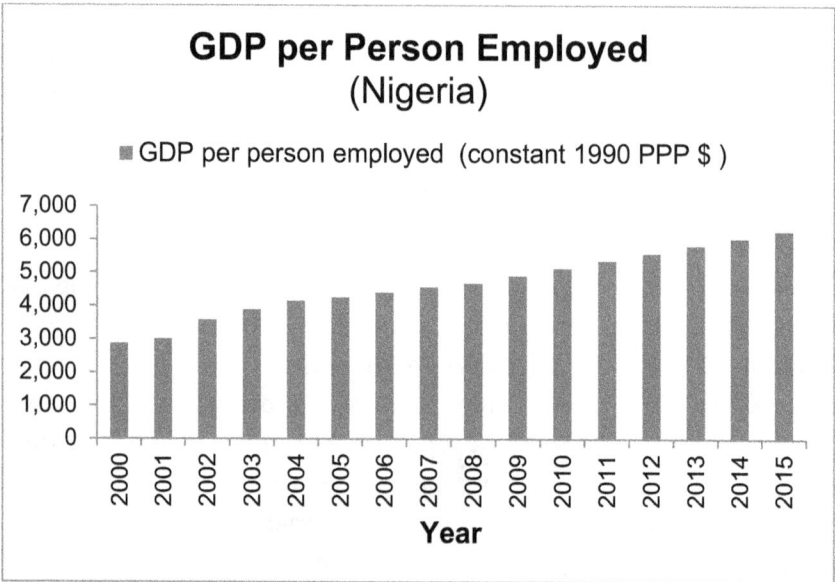

GDP per Person Employed (Nigeria)

▪ GDP per person employed (constant 1990 PPP $)

[Bar chart showing GDP per person employed values rising from about 2,900 in 2000 to about 6,100 in 2015, with bars for years 2000 through 2015. Y-axis scale: 0 to 7,000 in increments of 1,000. X-axis labeled "Year".]

GDP per Person Employed (2000-2015) in Nigeria. Source: International Labour Organization

In this example from Nigeria, although GDP per capita more than doubled (from $1,000 to over $2,000) in the last decade, GDP per person employed[68] was even higher (almost $5,000) in 2009. GDP per person employed represents people that are employed or are in the middle class. This figure could be significantly higher (up to $9,000), but a majority probably earn close to this figure. The data suggests that although unemployment is high, employed people are very productive and as a result have higher incomes than the general population.

---

[68] GDP per Person Employed is Gross Domestic Product (GDP) divided by Total Employment in the economy. Purchasing Power Parity (PPP) GDP is GDP converted to 1990 constant international dollars, using PPP rates. An international dollar has the same purchasing power over GDP that a U.S. Dollar has in the United States. Source: International Labour Organization, Key Indicators of the Labour Market database.

This means that the middle class in Nigeria is a good market for consumer goods. This class is made up of young urban professionals, who are employed in the service sector of the economy and are also entrepreneurs on the sidelines.

Insights for Investors

In this example from Nigeria, incomes have steadily increased over the years even in the absence of robust economic growth. Incomes for this market segment are not dependent on robust economic growth and will steadily rise even when growth is anemic.

For investors, this translates to a reliable and steady consumer market. They can also serve as a niche market for luxury and other uncommon goods.

Discovering Opportunities from Population Demographics

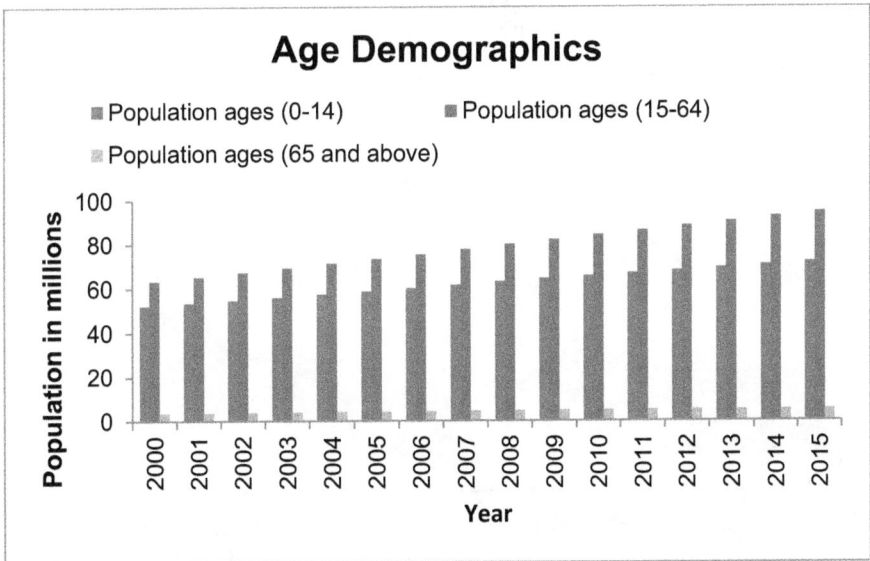

Age Demographics

■ Population ages (0-14)   ■ Population ages (15-64)
▨ Population ages (65 and above)

Population in millions (y-axis: 0, 20, 40, 60, 80, 100)

Year (x-axis: 2000, 2001, 2002, 2003, 2004, 2005, 2006, 2007, 2008, 2009, 2010, 2011, 2012, 2013, 2014, 2015)

Population by Age Range. Source: World Bank/United Nations

In this example from Nigeria, as of 2008 64 million (43%) Nigerians are between the ages of 0-14 years[69], 82 million (52%) Nigerians are between the ages of 15-64 years, and about 4 million Nigerians (3%) are 65 years and above.

Insights for Investors

Breaking down age demographics will provide insights into total market size for anything from cars to food. It also tells investors where to put their money – healthcare and pharmaceutical products for a country with a young population - for instance.

In this example from Nigeria, only about 3% of Nigerians are currently 65 years and above, this data suggests that Nigeria will have one of the largest ageing populations in the world thirty years from now. As the economy continues to do well and incomes increase, there will be a decline in birth rates and an increase in life expectancy. This will buoy this consumer class and create opportunities, especially in healthcare and pharmaceuticals, for businessmen who care to position themselves now.

It is an excellent guide for marketing strategy and knowing how to target each demographic.

---

[69] Population age ranges (0-14, 15-64, 65 and above) are percentages they each represent of the total population. Population is based on the de facto definition of population. Sources: World Bank staff estimates from various sources including census reports; the United Nations Population Division's World Population Prospects; national statistical offices; household surveys conducted by national agencies; and Macro International.

Discovering Opportunities in Inflation Data

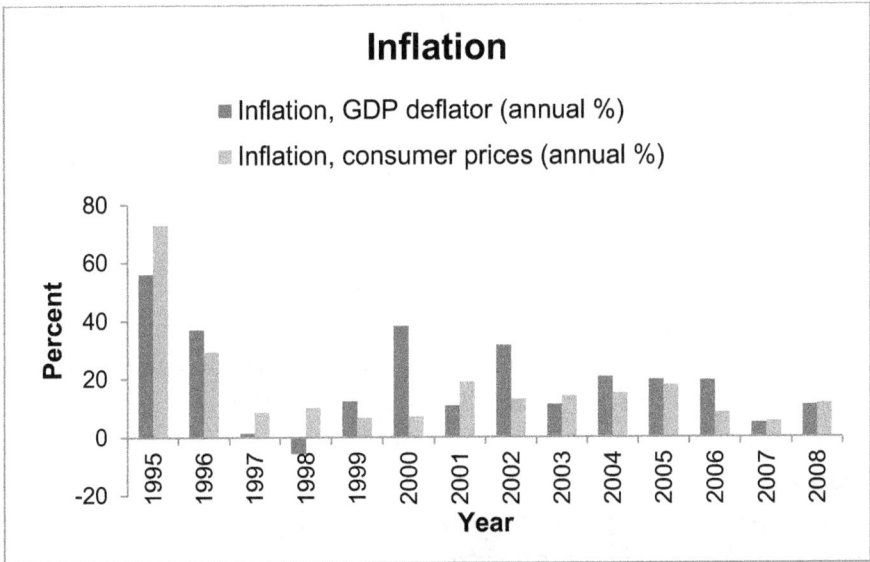

GDP Deflator and Consumer Prices Inflation (1995-2008). Source: OECD/International Monetary Fund/World Bank

As expected the GDP deflator[70], which is change in the general price level in the country, moves in tandem with consumer price inflation[71]. In this example from Nigeria, the inflation (consumer price) average for the 1990s was around 30% and in the last decade it hovered around 13%.

---

[70] Inflation as measured by the annual growth rate of the GDP implicit deflator shows the rate of price change in the economy as a whole. The GDP implicit deflator is the ratio of GDP in current local currency to GDP in constant local currency. Source: World Bank national accounts data and OECD National Accounts data files.

[71] Inflation as measured by the consumer price index reflects the annual percentage change in the cost to the average consumer of acquiring a basket of goods and services that may be fixed or changed at specified intervals, such as yearly. The Laspeyres formula is generally used. Source: International Monetary Fund, International Financial Statistics (including data files).

Improving inflation numbers in the past decade has translated to higher incomes, foreign and local investment, a larger economy, higher Internet usage among Nigerians, and a more liquid stock market. By and large, lower inflation numbers has increased the fortunes of the Nigerian economy.

Insights for Investors

In this example from Nigeria, better monetary management and inflation targeting, due to central bank reform in 2001, led to a lower inflation average (13%) in the last decade when compared to the 1990s when inflation averaged 25%.

Lower inflation, or better monetary management, drives investment. It is no surprise that the era of lower inflation coincided with higher economic growth and incomes. This has had a positive effect on stock market capitalization through the mechanism of better monetary management, spurring investment. Increased investment means economic growth which, in turn, means that investors/companies are making profit. This potentially drives individuals to invest in their stocks.

Lower inflation also increases savings because it enhances the purchasing power of money so that people are more confident to leave their money in the local currency, the Naira. This savings is pooled by financial institutions into loans to businesses and the stock market. Inflation also drives consumer credit provided by banks. This is because central banks usually inflate an economy (increase money supply or cheap credit) to grow it. So, inflation sometimes is synonymous with economic expansion and this usually works through banks extending credit to business.

The Nigerian (African) consumer has enjoyed a resurgence in the last decade because their incomes did not suffer the inflation erosion of the 1990s. This is a plus for demand and spending in the Nigerian economy.

Conclusion

Lessons learned from the Nigerian consumer markets can be applied to other African markets. The following factors will continue to drive consumers markets across Africa:

- Ongoing economic liberalization and reforms (finance, energy, land, power, petroleum subsidy, mining and tax)
- High commodity (agriculture and metals) prices in the international market
- Greater fiscal and monetary responsibility
- Regional trading blocs (COMESA, ECOWAS, etc.)
- Increasing trade with emerging Asia

Robust economic growth creates a middle class; a middleclass is all about a growing economy, investment, and jobs. Africa's middle class is no different from their counterparts worldwide. They:

- Want to acquire things like a house, cars, cell phones, etc.
- Want quality food like fast food outlets, packaged food, etc.
- Want quality clothing like designer labels and fashion
- Are hardworking and entrepreneurial

It's no surprise that the fortune of the middle class is tied to the growth of consumer markets. Consumers in this market have little, or no, debt overall and are living in a region where growth will significantly go up moving forward.

13

Recognizing and Leveraging New and Alternative Forms of Assets

Lauri Elliott

Once you have an understanding of the context for which you need to shape strategy and have started to look at some opportunities, you need to start developing a framework to shape the strategy. One framework for developing strategy is to focus on leverage points.

The Leverage Point Strategy™ is a specific methodology based on the concept of leverage. Leverage is the ratio of change in input to the change in output. Greater leverage is gained when a small force multiplies output. The goal is to see a small force produce as much change in output as possible.

Leverage points are those forces, or points, that create the rate of change in output. The power of leverage points is on a continuum from low to high. The best scenario is to locate high leverage points, because, in these cases, the smallest amounts of force effect the greatest change or results.

A very clear picture of a leverage point is the rudder of a ship. It is a small part of the ship in comparison with the size of the ship, but it creates a small force that is able to turn the ship in a new direction. In practical terms, maximizing leverage points makes use of small, but significant, forces.

Leverage points are related to tipping points. A tipping point is a point at which an object is displaced from one place to a new and different state. Leverage points are used to create the tipping point.

Malcolm Gladwell wrote the book *The Tipping Point: How Little Things Make a Big Difference*[72]. He identified three key factors, or types of leverage points, for creating tipping points: the Law of the Few, the Stickiness Factor, and the Power of Context.

The Law of the Few is when a few key types of people champion and catalyze an idea, or concept, to critical mass. The types of people are Connectors, Mavens, and Salesmen. When all three types of actors advocate an idea, the concept is more likely to reach a tipping point. Connectors, Mavens, and Salesmen are examples of leverage points. Each is a small force that can wield significant results.

The Stickiness Factor is something that sticks in the minds of individuals and influences their behavior in the future. And the Power of Context is when the right environment, or time, aligns with your business opportunity to create momentum.

Each of the leverage points highlighted by Gladwell can induce a tipping point, but it is more likely that the combination of these leverage points will actually force a tipping point.

Another category of leverage points is types of capital. In essence, these are the strengths you bring to the business opportunity overall. According to Dr. Bruce Cook of Kingdom Venture Capital, there are 13 types of capital:

- **Economic** includes currency, liquid assets, and finance.
- **Social** includes community-focused or social good activities, such as relief work, charity, and scientific research.
- **Spiritual** refers to strength drawn from faith and your internal spirit.
- **Knowledge** is what you and your team know, both the intellectual and mental processes.
- **Political** refers to formal political affiliations and influence.

---

[72] Gladwell, M. (2002). *The Tipping Point: How Little Things Make a Big Difference.* New York, NY: Back Bay Books (Hatchette Book Group).

- **Environmental** refers to assets in the global "green" movement, like carbon credits.
- **Creative** includes your creativity, artistic expression, and intellectual property.
- **Positional** refers to the roles, titles, and authority you hold both formally and informally.
- **Institutional** includes formal reputation, influence, status, alliances, and partners.
- **Physical** refers to your body's capacity, including energy and fitness.
- **Generational** refers to legacy, heritage, family lineage, and wealth that are passed down in families.
- **Closeness** refers to the ability to draw close and also to be vulnerable, or open, in relationships.
- **Relational** refers to the span and depth of your relationships both vertically and horizontally.

You may wonder how some types of capital (e.g., social) can serve as leverage points for business, but any form of capital can exert influence over business opportunities. For example, a young African-American attorney, Carlton Owens, moved to Ghana and established a gold mine. His gold mine sits on land on which a local indigenous tribe lives. In addition to getting a mining concession from the government, he had to form an agreement with the local chief on how the operation would benefit the community beyond jobs. Carlton agreed to build a school, among other things. In emerging markets, business is not separated from the complex system of society.

In actuality, many things are leverage points, including situations and circumstances. However, the leverage point might be in your favor or in someone else's, and the leverage point may have low or high impact. Your goal is to find a series of leverage points in your favor with high-impact potential.

The process of applying the Leverage Point Strategy™ works in conjunction with completing an environmental analysis, as well as a SWOT analysis, of your opportunities. Following these analyses, apply the Leverage Point Strategy™ by asking yourself the following questions:

- What are the key leverage points that will make an opportunity work?
- Which of the key leverage points have high, medium, or low impact?
- Which combinations of key leverage points will have the most impact?
- How will the key leverage points help to override the weaknesses and threats in an opportunity?
- In general, how will I incorporate the high-leverage points and high-leverage-point combinations into the business model?
- How will I know if the leverage points are working?

Once you have applied the Leverage Point Strategy™ to your analysis of opportunities, incorporate the leverage points into your business model appropriately. The business model gives a complete picture of how to implement the business successfully. It answers the question, "How do you logically create value?" Johan Wallin, in the book *Business Orchestration: Strategic Leadership in the Era of Digital Convergence*[73], says a business model:

> ...*defines the value-creation priorities of an actor (business) in respect to the utilization of both internal and external resources. It defines how the actor (business) relates with stakeholders, such as actual and potential customers, employees, unions, suppliers, competitors and other internal groups. It takes account of situations where the actor's (business') activities may (a) affect the business environment and its own business in ways that create*

---

[73] Wallin, J. (2006). *Business Orchestration: Strategic Leadership in the Era of Digital Convergence.* New York, NY: Wiley.

conflicting interests, or impose risks on the actor (business) or (b) develop new, previously unpredicted ways of creating value.

In the book *Business Model Generation: A Handbook for Visionaries, Game Changers, and Challengers*[74], Alexander Osterwalder and Yves Pigneur pose key questions to consider when developing a solid business model. The following is an adaptation focused on leverage points: "What key leverage points will you use to…"

- Activate your customer segments?
- Maximize your revenue streams?
- Improve offerings for your customer segments?
- Better relate to your customers over time?
- Maximize resource allocation to run the business?
- Improve efficiency and effectiveness of key activities in running the business?
- Better utilize and leverage the "people" assets used to run the business?
- Increase and improve outputs of key activities?
- Maximize partnerships, alliances, and collaboration?
- Maximize network and distribution channels to reach customers?
- Manage and reduce costs of running the business?

Leverage points are simply tangible and intangible assets, resources, situations, etc. that can be used to gain and sustain momentum in the business environment. As you analyze a business opportunity, or problem, identify leverage points. And, use leverage points to help you assess opportunities, as well as incorporate the best leverage points and combinations into the business model and operations.

---

[74] Osterwalder, A., & Pigneur, Y. (2010). *Business Model Generation: A Handbook for Visionaries, Game Changers, and Challengers*. New York, NY: Wiley.

Faith Networks – An Example of an Underutilized Asset

There is an under tapped channel to catalyze trade and economic development in Africa. It has existed for hundreds of years. Today, it readily and effectively responds to disaster after disaster around the world. It is a part of the civil society sphere, which is considered vital to a functioning society. This channel is faith networks. Here we will consider the Christian faith network.

In Africa, there are close to 500 million Christians and 400 million Muslims. These numbers account for 90% of the entire population.

The Christian faith is predominant in Sub-Saharan Africa. So, if you want to reach out to Africans in this region for any reason, it's logical to tap the Christian faith network.

Some may have a hard time with this because in the West there is a vocal credo of the "separation of church and state" whether it is truly legislated or really works is another issue. For example, it is known that when disaster strikes in the United States the National Voluntary Active Disaster (Vo-ad) network, comprised mostly of faith-related institutions, is a fast and effective responder. In fact, the Federal Emergency Management Agency (FEMA) in the United States signed a memorandum of understanding with Vo-ad to reach out to communities in disaster. In Haiti, there were already many faith organizations like Operation Blessing there and able to tap into their global networks to ramp up response.

And, if the truth be told, government and international aid organizations partner with local faith organizations to reach local populations in the developing world. Why? First, they understand and have become in varying degrees part of the local culture and people. Second, faith culture in developing nations is one of the most powerful social institutions.

Third, the Christian faith network has a way of reaching people even in very remote regions. Some Christian pastors and bishops establish churches in rural and remote regions. To reach these communities, they may have to walk or ride a motorcycle, but they do reach them.

So, if the Christian faith network can help address natural disasters, why can't they be tapped to address an even larger, continual disaster – poverty in Africa? To the audience that finds it hard to mix business and faith, poverty or untapped wealth in Africa is a continual disaster that needs to be addressed. From an economic standpoint, until Africa is able to tap its wealth more broadly there will continue to be an overreliance on aid.

In actuality, faith-based organizations already support economic development. Professor Nwabufo Uzodike, Head of the School of Politics at the University of KwaZulu-Natal, reports that the Catholic Church has stepped in to assist communities with economic development projects in the DRC because of insufficient government institutions. Also, large international aid organizations like World Vision embed economic development components in their community development projects.

Other faith-based organizations like Business Partners International and the Center for Entrepreneurship at Regent University's School of Business help develop small and medium enterprises in developing countries. In these instances, however, the goal is to serve the people by helping them get out of poverty.

What is not activated is positioning the Christian faith network as a market and economy. If we look at the aid sector, Western businesses already tap large aid, faith or non-faith, organizations as clients. So, in some realms this is already working, but at the same time the "aid" engine is perverted in certain ways making some wealthy and keeping others in poverty. A friend of mine worked for a large U.S.-based aid organization focused on refugees in parts of Africa. She suggested that they help the refugees develop enterprises. She was told matter-of-factly they would not do so because it would put the organization out of business.

In a good example, CARE decided to no longer participate in some aspects of the World Food Programme (WFP) because they were not able to leverage their assets to catalyze economic opportunities as much for the communities they served. Through WFP, CARE might be paying more to foreign firms for what local businesses could supply more affordably. By re-focusing supply chains to local entrepreneurs, CARE helps create more opportunities and can help stimulate local economies.

Fortunately, the traditional development formula may be changing in small ways, at least in the U.S. since one of the pillars of its development assistance is to catalyze sustainable economic growth. The Kauffman Foundation has even proposed using military resources to catalyze local economic development in post-conflict zones. Kauffman calls this "expeditionary" economics.

But beyond the argument for helping people get out of poverty is the importance of pulling people out of poverty for the global economy so everyone wins. Dambisa Moyo, author of *Dead Aid*[75], popularized the stance of "trade instead of aid" for Africa. While aid is helpful for development, it is not a sustainable solution.

And until this balances out, developed countries will likely continue to pour out aid to assist. These are the same countries who are reeling under debt like the U.S. and U.K. At some point, if there isn't a shift in this system, like the world financial systems, it will reel out of control and break, leaving more destruction in its path.

Trade, markets, and business, on the other hand, are the engines of thriving economies. Africa's poverty is systemic, so a systematic solution is needed not just pockets of solutions.

First, we need to identify and leverage existing systems that have enough momentum to catalyze economic opportunity. Second, we need to find ways to catalyze trade within these networks in Africa to create wealth instead of poverty, reducing reliance on aid.

Faith and business have co-existed for hundreds of years in Africa. The Islamic faith spread through Arab traders in Africa. While Christianity started in North Africa and Ethiopia many centuries before Islam, it did not spread into Sub-Saharan Africa in a major way until Europeans came to the continent. It is now time to activate this channel as a market, or economy to benefit many.

The Christian faith network is organized in local, regional, and global spaces, which can perhaps be considered markets not just faith communities or organizations. For example, local churches are normally

---

[75] Moyo, D. (2010). Dead Aid: Why Aid is Not Working and How There is a Better Way for Africa. New York, NY: Farrar, Straus & Giroux.

under the leadership of a geographic administration, which in turn is connected to state, national, and international church administrations. There are also often direct connections between churches in developed nations to those in developing nations, focusing on specific projects like building schools, houses, and hospitals.

It also should be noted that, in the United States, faith is a specific market segment. There is a very strong Christian marketplace, including music, messages, books, etc. CBA, a Christian retail sector association, estimated that in 2006 Christian sales through its members exceeded $4.6 billion. This doesn't include sales in mainstream bookstores and discounters like Barnes and Noble and Wal-Mart. So, faith and the marketplace do mix. Why can't the social networks in the Christian faith network be leveraged for other economic pursuits on a more systematic and global scale, connecting one community at a time?

The Christian faith network can also bring a transformed ethical framework, trust, and emphasis on people into the alternative market constructed around them. And, if anything, the importance of these factors in the wake of the global economic crisis should be self-evident.

Leveraging Faith Networks in Agriculture

So how would something like this work? One of the best markets to consider is agriculture because of Africa's ability to be a major agricultural consumer and producer. Africa has a growing population, increasing the demand for agricultural products.

In fact, agricultural production in Africa has the potential to serve world markets as well. The importance of agriculture to the world was felt with the food shortages and price spikes in the last several years. This has ignited greater interest in the agricultural sector, particularly in Africa which has a lot of virgin, arable land. The purchase of African land for agricultural development by foreign investors and governments is a normal occurrence now.

Unfortunately, the agricultural sector in Africa faces challenges, including low crop yields, distribution, and access to world markets, giving a very different picture. However, some improvements in the value chain have made a significance difference as was illustrated by the example of Malawi in *Chapter 6: Agriculture.*

If the U.S. Christian church turns its attention to this opportunity, there are consumers, businesses, and investors within this faith community that could tie into the African agricultural sector. Christian businessmen, specializing in agriculture and related sectors, could develop and/or invest in African agricultural projects for profit. U.S. Christians can take advantage of AGOA (to export products from Africa to U.S.) and other U.S. programs.

The Christian church can also tie these business opportunities to communities they serve or provide aid to in Africa, helping develop sustainable livelihoods. This includes marketing, distributing, and selling the products among their networks. As an example, the Christian Reformed World Relief Committee advocates purchasing Fair Trade products.

Again, it's not that pieces of this puzzle are not already working in varying degrees, but it's not configured as a market or economy to leverage and maximize existing assets within it to benefit the broadest number of members in the Christian faith network whether in Africa or elsewhere. If it does represent a market or economy, it is fragmented.

And finally, while there are significant challenges and obstacles to taking this approach, the Christian faith network has many leverage points working in its favor, including existing infrastructure to distribute information and resources, funding for seeding agricultural projects which will bring a return on investment, and most of all, ecosystems of people who have the knowledge and expertise to make it happen.

Conclusion

There can be no question that traditional ways of looking at assets and capital are reasons why many opportunities lie fallow. As we speak of innovation in technology, we also need to look at how to innovate the raw materials, both tangible and intangible, that we have and to which we have access to.

Cultural networks are a way of life in Africa, and they also represent channels through which business is done. The Christian faith network is one of those networks that have an extensive reach on the continent both in urban and rural areas, as well as formal and informal marketplaces.

The Christian faith network represents a unique network to leverage because on many variables it already has the resources – people on the ground, local knowledge and connections, funding, facilities, distribution channels, etc. The key is to transform use of these resources for economic development through broad-based, for-profit ventures.

14

Economic and Trade Leverage Points
Lauri Elliott

As mentioned in the previous chapters almost any variable can be seen through the lens of leverage points. However, it is always good to have a core set of leverage points you can look at when shaping strategy for Africa, or other emerging markets. This chapter will discuss three leverage points designed to accelerate and sustain broad-based economic development and trade, but are also tools businesses can leverage for their own ventures.

Economic Zones and Clusters

Economic zones are geographic areas designated to promote trade and economic development within a country. They tend to have more liberalized economic policies than the countries in which they reside, and these policies are highly conducive to both native and foreign business. Typical advantages for businesses and investors include tax incentives, better infrastructure, better institutions, better processes, and freer flow of international trade.

There are different forms of economic zones, from free ports to information-processing zones. Some economic zones around the globe include Hyderabad, New Delhi, and Pune in India; Subic and Bataan in the Philippines; and Dubna and Lipetsk in Russia.

China's growth story is very tied to the introduction of economic zones in the 1980s. For example, the Shenzhen Export Processing Zone was a small village and has now grown to almost the size of a megacity with around 9 million people.

Not only are economic zones often better places to conduct business, but they may also offer the chance of a growing market for businesses. The

Africa Free Zone Association (AFZA)[76] maintains a partial list of free zones in Africa.

Another model for concentrating and leveraging economic activity is clusters, most notably researched and introduced by Michael Porter. A cluster is a group of enterprises in close geographic proximity that produce similar or related products in a particular field – e.g., nanotechnology, leather, diamonds, etc. In Uganda, there are over 20 diverse clusters under development.

Globally, nations are seeing clusters as a means to spur economic development. For businesses, they may offer alliances, bringing expertise, value chains, and capacity, in a foreign country.

One of the models for economic clusters is Silicon Valley in San Jose, California. This technology cluster has created an ecosystem that drives technology innovation around the globe. Note that successful clusters also can spur connections with other markets and multinationals, such as the case with the automotive clusters in India. In the Chennai-Hosur-Bangalore region cluster, Toyota, Mitsubishi, Hyundai and Ford are among the multinationals involved.

In essence, economic zones and clusters serve as pathways for global businesses to enter new markets through the inherent strengths they bring. A business can find expertise and ecosystems to support its singular effort to enter new markets while containing the strain on existing resources.

While country analysis is important for assessing an opportunity, taking a closer look at the strengths of specific economic zones or clusters within a country may help you discover leverage points in favor of doing business in that country even when the overall country analysis indicates that the business climate there is weak. To flesh out your understanding of using economic zones and clusters as leverage points, consider the questions on the following page:

---

[76] http://www.afzaonline.com

- What economic clusters or zones exist in the emerging economy of interest?
- Which economic clusters or zones align with your business strategy?
- What is the experience of others in the economic cluster or zone of interest?
- Are there other companies from your country present or involved in the economic cluster or zone?
- What incentives are provided in the economic zone? How does this improve the opportunity for you?
- At what stage of development is the economic cluster or zone? Is its development sufficient to prove useful to you?
- What is the rate of increased economic activity and population around the economic zone or cluster? Is this in itself a market to consider?
- Can you offer services or products that are needed by firms in an economic zone or cluster?
- Are there firms with which you can partner or align in the economic zone or cluster?

Regional Economic Communities

Like economic hubs, regional economic communities (RECs) can provide a strategic focus for businesses and investors. RECs focus on creating at least a free trade area, customs union, and common market between member countries. While this helps the member countries with cross-border trade and opens markets to the world, it also provides larger and more varied opportunities for businesses and investors.

The European Union (EU) is a prime example. The *World Factbook* says the population of the EU was over 500 million in 2010, compared with about 85 million in Germany, its most populated member state. The purchasing power of 500 million people would obviously be greater than that of 85 million in most cases.

The goal of an REC is to make the movement of factors of production, as well as goods and services, between member countries as easy as within the countries. This will guarantee efficient resource use, which is a competitiveness factor that can attract investment and boost economic growth. For businesses and entrepreneurs, it means that a free trade agreement in the REC will allow your products to move from one country to another with few or no tariffs and make it easier for you to reach across borders within the region to expand your market.

As an example, if you planned to concentrate your business and investment ventures in the East Africa economic hub of Kenya, you would greatly benefit from the ICT infrastructure and institutions developed for the East Africa Community (EAC)[77]. The EAC consists of Burundi, Kenya, Rwanda, Tanzania, and Uganda. It has a combined population of about 136 million, compared with about 40 million in Kenya alone. For those who do business and invest in consumer markets, the difference in market potential based on size is significant.

RECs can also help businesses more successfully navigate within many countries simultaneously by harmonizing policies, incentives, etc., between member states. For example, the EAC is working on a regional investment code, which means foreign businesses and investors will have one code to engage with, as opposed to five.

In summary, RECs enlarge market potential for businesses automatically and can make it easier to navigate business in several countries simultaneously. However, it is important to identify the specific benefits and limitations of an REC in the case of your opportunities. As you explore RECs as leverage points, consider the following questions:

- In which regional economic communities, or free trade agreements, does the emerging market of interest participate?
- What are the market size and characteristics of the regional economic community for your sector and industry?
- What additional opportunities does the regional economic community bring to you?

---

[77] For more details on RECs in Africa, access
http://www.afribiz.info/content/afribiz-may-2009-focusing-on-regional-economic-communities-to-successfully-do-business-in-africa.

- Does your country have direct agreements with the regional economic community?
- What other trade agreements does the regional economic community have with other countries or regions? How can you benefit from those?
- In which country in the regional economic community should you start?
- How can you use regional economic communities to leverage your other strengths?
- Can you consult other firms from your country that are doing a lot of business in the regional economic community?
- What is the economic outlook for the regional economic community in question?
- What factors – e.g., tariffs, border crossing, and transport – within the regional economic community still present challenges for cross-border trade? How can you work around them?

Trade and Investment Agreements

A trade agreement is one between two or more parties, possibly covering a wide range of tax, tariff, trade, and investment issues. In bilateral agreements between two countries like Canada and South Africa, there are preferential and protection measures that benefit businesses from both countries. Along with trade agreements, business councils are mandated by governments to represent the private sector. In some sense, they are similar to chambers of commerce.

Businesses can incorporate the preferential and protection measures in trade agreements to leverage opportunities in a specific country. Typical concerns of those doing business overseas include the following: How easy is it to remove money from the host country? What protection is there for assets in the host country? These and other issues may be covered by trade or investment agreements.

Trade agreements also bring opportunities to network, since businesses generally form part of the diplomatic delegations accompanying government officials to discuss trade agreements. For example, President

Jacob Zuma of South Africa recently took along over 350 businesspeople on his state visit to China. This offers businesses unique access to people and organizations in the host country.

Also, business councils serve as excellent channels to gain information, contacts, and expertise on operating in a foreign country. In a recent example, I had a person approach me who needed very specific information about getting a product through customs in Algeria. I contacted the U.S.-Algeria Business Council, and they were readily able to identify the organization that could assist. For someone trying to retrieve this information on his or her own, the process could have taken several weeks.

The United Nations Conference on Trade and Development (UNCTAD) keeps a list of bilateral and investment agreements in place for each country. However, you can check with the foreign affairs ministry or department in your country, as well as investment and promotion agencies.

Trade agreements can serve as key leverage points, owing to the ecosystems developed to support them. However, you will need to explore any trade agreement in sufficient detail so that you understand its benefits, limitations, and implications. While you are exploring trade and investment agreements as leverage points, consider the following questions:

- What trade agreements does your country hold with countries in Africa?
- What aspect of those trade agreements can you leverage for your business?
- What protection does the trade agreement offer?
- Are there any initiatives developed through the trade agreement in which you should be involved?
- Are there business opportunities arising out of initiatives evolving from the trade agreement?
- What business opportunities have been identified for businesses in your home country through the trade agreement?
- Who are the key stakeholders of whom you should be aware?
- Which trade agreements tied to the host country will also help your business enter other markets?

- Who can you consult that has intimate knowledge of the trade agreements?
- How will specific trade agreements allow you to leverage other strengths?

Conclusion

As Africa grows as a global business, investment, and trade hub, there will be any number of facilities to conduct business with the continent. It is important to stay abreast of key trade and economic mechanisms that will assist your business.

These mechanisms, or leverage points, serve as tangible and intangible assets in your network that you can leverage. Even though you do not have the internal capacity or capital of multinational firms, leverage points like these allow you to operate as a micro-multinational – a small global firm, operating in more than one country.

15

Leveraging Trust Networks
Lauri Elliott

On any day, you will find people exchanging things of value. A typical picture is a person buying a product from a vendor with cash or credit. However, value can be exchanged in a variety of ways including exchanges of information, services, resources, and products. Exchanges happen between individuals, businesses, organizations, and governments at inconceivable rates of speed, particularly with the advent of electronic payment systems and the Internet.

While the idea of exchanging value may be a simple concept, it is played out in a complex environment. For example, the value chain to deliver cars to customers involves an entire ecosystem of agents, people, and organizations. There are the designers and engineers that draw the blueprint for the car. There are firms that transform raw materials into parts. There are other firms that take parts and transform them into components. Then, there are firms that assemble the vehicles. And consider the transport, distribution, and sales systems which support the entire value chain.

One common denominator in all forms of value exchange is trust. Both sides of the exchange trust they are getting the value expected from the exchange, trusting each other to provide the value expected or agreed upon. According to Merriam-Webster, trust is the "assured reliance on the character, ability, strength, or truth of someone or something."

Kenneth Arrow, an international economist, said as economic and social interactions become more complex, trust becomes the lubricant to keep things moving.[78] Oil lubricates engine parts to reduce friction between

---

[78] Arrow, K. (1974). *Limits of Organization.* New York: W.W. Norton & Company.

moving parts while improving efficiency and reducing wear, trust does similarly for business transactions, markets, and economic systems.

Anthony Giddens said that as societal and organizational processes modernize trust also becomes more important.[79] Georg Simmel suggests that individual and collective wealth would not exist today without trust.[80]

If trust is so important to economic interaction, can it be used to leverage global business opportunities? And if so, how can it be used?

In fact, trust is already leveraged to take advantage of global business opportunities. The example that affects all of us is "fiat" money. Fiat money, which is typically thought of as paper but also includes coins, is currency which a government decrees is legal tender. Fiat money has no intrinsic value but we trust the government issuing the currency is backed by something of value.

We can look to the recent example of Zimbabwe to see when fiat money is not backed by something of value and a government is not trusted to deliver something of value against it. Zimbabwe experienced hyperinflation in the latter half of the first decade of the 21st century. The Zimbabwean government continued to print more bank notes without any evidence they were backed by something of value. At one point in 2009, the government planned to issue different denominations of (e.g. 10, 50) trillion Zimbabwean dollar notes, which would have been valued well below $100.

More and more businesses and people began to use foreign currency, refusing to accept Zimbabwe's local currency. People even exchanged mobile phone minute scratch cards as a form of currency. They no longer trusted in Zimbabwe's legal tender. In the end, Zimbabwe stopped circulation of its local currency and the U.S. Dollar and South African Rand became the country's legal tender, along (theoretically) with the Euro and the British Pound.

---

[79] Giddens, A. (1990). *The Consequences of Modernity.* Stanford, CA: Stanford University Press.
[80] Simmel, G. (1978). *The Philosophy of Money.* London: Routledge & Kegan Paul.

This example illustrates trust at work in major systems, but there are many practical examples in everyday business. A manager who delegates tasks to sub-ordinates, but then micromanages them, does not trust them. Micromanagement leads to de-motivation and bad team dynamics, which ultimately will cost.

There are other ways that trust can be leveraged to do global business. Research has shown that trust improves negotiations, increases flow of information, increases ability to learn, increases flexibility in management, increases speed of business transactions, and reduces costs, such as costs of transaction, governing relationships, agency, and opportunity.[81]

Trust is actually a strategic resource, according to Jay Barney and Mark Hansen, and can lead to competitive advantage when strong trust exists.[82] But more than a resource that can be used up and depleted, it is a strategic asset that if developed and managed correctly will only grow.

Imagine being a firm whose partners and customers always come back for more, are loyal, and help build business by word of mouth. In this scenario, both your tangible and intangible assets rise. This can create a unique niche for you in the market. Apple has consistently delivered to its customers, so they keep coming for more.

Unfortunately, trust is seen as an intangible versus a tangible by most, leading to the perception that building it, managing it, and leveraging it is a shot in the dark. However, according to Steven Covey in the *Speed of Trust*[83], this is far from the truth. Covey says that there are 13 behaviors of high-trust leaders, including showing loyalty, talking straight, creating transparency, and delivering results.

---

[81] Bachmann, R., & Zaheer, A. (eds.) (2006). *Handbook of Trust Research.* Cheltenham, UK: Edward Elgar Publishing.

[82] Barney, J.B., & Hansen, M.H. (1994). Trustworthiness as a Source of Competitive Advantage. *Strategic Management Journal, 15,* 175-190.

[83] Covey, M.R. (2008). *The Speed of Trust: The One Thing that Changes Everything.* New York, NY: Free Press (Simon & Schuster).

To manage the "how" of leveraging trust in business, there must be a sufficient framework to apply. Covey presents different spheres of trust as the "Five Waves of Trust". The first wave (Self-Trust) is to trust yourself. The second wave (Relationship Trust) is trust others.

The third through fifth waves represent "systems" of trust, including organizational, market, and societal. Covey refers to these "systems" of trust as Stakeholder Trust. Organizational Trust (the third wave) focuses on internal stakeholders while Market and Societal Trust (the fourth and fifth waves) focus on external stakeholders.

Covey's concept of Stakeholder Trust is on target, but it bypasses the dynamic, fluid, and complex nature of these systems. Covey's perspective does not adequately address inter-organizational/inter-market systems like joint ventures, alliances, partnerships, and value chains, which dominate the business environment today. Yet, trust is the vital center for coordinating interaction in such systems, according to Bill McEvily, Vincenzo Perrone, and Akbar Zabeer.[84]

Another perspective, which accounts for the dynamic, fluid, and complex nature of stakeholder systems, is thinking of them as networks. A simple definition of a network is an interconnected system of things or people.

Networks are composed of nodes and their relationships. In people networks like markets, the nodes are people. The key questions for these networks are: 1) Who are the people? 2) How are they related? and 3) What do these relationships exchange and produce?

The concept of networks frames the business context in which trust plays a key role. Networks can frame organizations, industries, value chains, and markets. These are systems designed to create or increase value to its stakeholders. So when we speak of business or economic systems, we are speaking of "value" networks. "Value networks is any web of relationship that generates both intangible and tangible value through complex,

---

[84] McEvily, B., Perrone, V., & Zabeer, A. (2003). Trust as an organizing principle. *Organization Science, 14*(1), 91-103.

dynamic exchanges between two or more individuals, groups, or organizations," according to Verna Allee of Value Networks.[85] This describes the networks that surround business and economic systems to a tee.

In actuality, trust and value brought by agents to an exchange both impact the exchange, but there aren't clear, precise boundaries for how these two elements interact, influence each other, and impact exchanges. For business, it's enough to know that trust can be leveraged for global business and that there are practical, simple ways to do so within the context of what I call "trust" networks.

A trust network is an overlay for a value network. The degree and type of trust that exists between people is one factor in determining what value they are willing to exchange and how they view and work in the relationship. So, as mentioned previously, trust has the central vital role for coordinating economic and value interactions and exchanges. Simply put, use trust to guide, organize, and manage your global business opportunities.

The concept of a trust network is not entirely new. On the web, in a similar fashion, trust networks exist. They are used so people can declare who they trust so others can see. There are other similar networks like reputation, which are normal for marketplaces and payment systems like Amazon, eBay, and PayPal. Users who have more people who trust them or uphold their reputation tend to draw business their way.

The power of trust networks is that anyone can put them to use for business. You don't need a certain amount of money, connections (a lot of people have connections that do not have high trust), information, and resources. As you work the methodology of trust networks, these things naturally come as you build the right flows to achieve business success.

---

[85] http://www.valuenetworks.com

Steps for Building a Trust Network for Global Business

One of the key misperceptions of going global is that you have to grow into it, developing enough capital resources to take on foreign markets. In reality, with the advent of telecommunications, the Internet, and technology, the cost of doing business globally can be a lot lower and within the budget and capacity of entrepreneurs and SMEs. Today, the resources that you can tap into, along with your own assets, shape your business opportunities. Hence, the importance of networks, particularly those built on trust, is evident because they allow you to tap into additional resources you do not have on your own.

Going global for an entrepreneur, or SME, can be costly, risky, and time consuming if done on his or her own. However, when you bring trusted associates into the equation, they can help spread the risk and reduce the time and cost to market.

Trust networks for global business start with the social and business networks an individual already has. An individual or organization works with "trusted" associates, configuring business strategy around the trust relationships and the information, resources, people, and capital they bring along with them.

The first step is to identify people within your formal, or informal, social and business networks to see who you trust. These are individual trust relationships. Openly talk about your business interests. It is often in these dialogues that opportunities appear.

The second step is to "chain" the individual trust relationships into a single, or a few, business opportunities. This results in a trust value chain to implement a business venture. If you choose the right trust relationships and opportunity frame, you can use this same chain over and over again to provide additional products and services to the same target market. The image on the following page illustrates a trust value chain.

Value Chain

Phase 1

Product Purchased (US)	Product Sold (NG)

Taylor
(US – RSA)

Ibez
(RSA - NG)

Susan
(US)

Emeka
(NG)

Investment
Supply

Local Operations
Sales

Proposed Ownership
Susan – 20%
Ibez, Taylor – 10%
Emeka – 70%

Facilitation
Coordination
Business Administration

Tangible Flow
Trust Flow

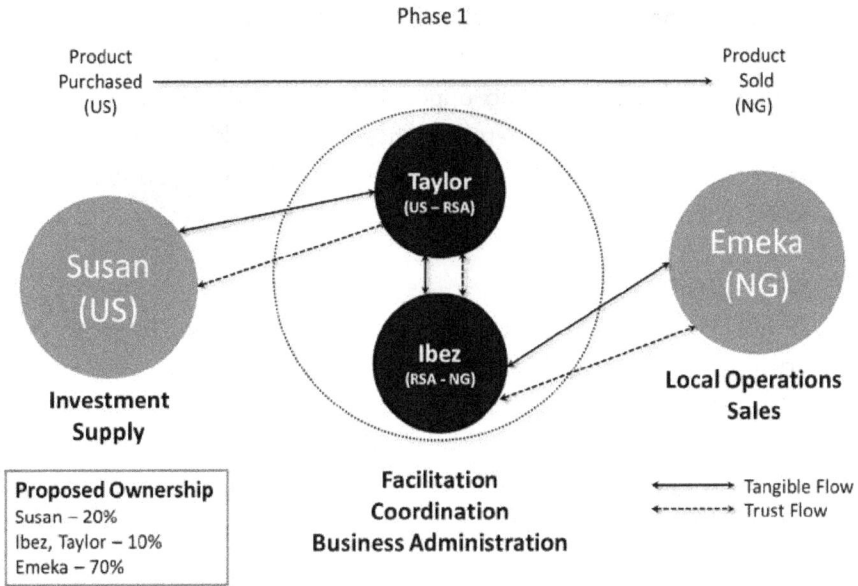

Source: Lauri Elliott

In dealing with any global business opportunity, but in the context of Africa, it is recommended to work with people you trust locally. You cannot micromanage, nor should you, from a distance. So, trust value chains are one method for conducting business. This method allows quick and effective action with business opportunities.

For example, we recently identified a product in the United States that would be highly useful in Africa. Because we are familiar with the local markets, we have identified several sectors and consumers that would readily use the quality product. We didn't spend a lot of time in feasibility because we could enter the market for little cost and allow it to grow. However, to make it work, we identified a small investor and supplier from the U.S. to manage purchasing the product and someone locally in Africa to sell it. These were identified and established through individual relationships.

In another example, we used trust to improve the effectiveness of a project. In a recent experience, we re-configured a new venture by placing a point of contact between two key stakeholders that both of them trusted.

And the third step is to repeat steps 1 and 2 to establish a trust network, which multiplies the economic opportunities and growth for everyone involved. In the dynamics of networks, healthy networks will become alive and grow on their own. But you have to start with strategic intent, not a haphazard approach.

Trust is a Strategic Asset

As mentioned earlier, trust is also a strategic asset. It's important to view your trust network not only as a vehicle to do business globally, but more so as assets that can grow and increase in value themselves if managed well. Not doing so is probably the primary downfall of any trust network. Individuals in the network begin to take the people and relationships for granted and not putting in the proper care to make sure the network remains healthy.

It's important to realize what it means for someone to trust you. That person is willing to become vulnerable to you with the expectation that you will not harm him or her through intention or behavior. In business, that person or organization is expecting you to look out for his or her interest as well as your own.

The trust relationship established with someone is not the only sphere to consider when managing a trust network. You also need to acknowledge the impact and influence created on spheres within business, community, and society.

Individual trust relationships directly impact and influence organizations to which those in the trust relationship belong. For example, the information exchange between two people in different organizations, as a part of a joint venture, can help both organizations become more competitive in the market. On the other hand, a consultant (advising a technology company), who learns the details of a new technology roll-out, and shares these details with outsiders so they can buy or sell stock in anticipation of this move, violates the trust the technology company placed in the consultant.

This last example has broader implications because it gives the stock traders unfair advantage over others, who might choose to buy or sell the stock. And, this type of breach of trust is actually against the law. The consultant has bankrupted his trust asset base just in this one act.

So, as you manage your portfolio of assets to grow wealth, you do the same with trust assets.

Building Trust in Individual Relationships

Since individuals are the lowest common denominator in a trust network, they should be seen as the essential building blocks for a trust network. As an individual, you need to consider both how you trust yourself and how you trust others. Healthy high-trust relationships can only be developed when individuals are able to trust themselves and willing to trust others. When considering your position in trust relationships, you should ask and address the following questions:

- Do you trust yourself to operate with integrity?
- Do you trust yourself to bear good intentions to others who trust you?
- Do you trust that you have the capacity to carry out what is asked of you? Within which boundaries, do you trust your capacity?
- Do you trust yourself to get results?
- Are you more prone to trust or distrust others?

Individuals inherently trust themselves and others in some instances and distrust in other instances. A few ways to engender trust within yourself:

- Learn to operate within the strengths and value you bring. Keep from being drawn into situations where you know you can't deliver.
- Only promise what you feel comfortable delivering.
- Deliver more than you promise.
- Don't be too critical of yourself. Be willing to forgive your own faults.

To engender trust within individual trust relationships, do the following:

- Listen more and when you do speak, speak plainly and straightforward.
- Show respect and deference for others.
- Be transparent as appropriate.
- Make yourself accountable to others and hold others accountable.
- Clarify expectations and keep commitments.
- Work on making relationships better.
- Be loyal.
- Correct mistakes or wrongdoings.
- Be alert for conflicts of interest and make others aware when they exist.
- Become vulnerable to the other person in the trust relationship.
- Share or give something to the other person in the trust relationship that they would value without asking for anything back.
- Keep someone's secrets whether or not they ask you to.
- If you make a mistake, whether you are caught or not, confess at the appropriate time and venue and ask for forgiveness.
- Be willing to lay down your interests for the interests of others when called for.

Applying Trust in Business Scenarios

In business, people tend to mostly think of the value others bring when entering agreements. That is the first decision point, but the second decision point, and often the final decision point, should be do you trust the person?

If you have any qualms on trusting the person at any level, you need to configure the agreement so that you are comfortable with the level of trust you are placing in the person. For example, a person has performed well for others previously, but your project has a much larger scale. If possible, split the project between two persons if you cannot find one person with which you feel comfortable.

And there are other times, when you have to stretch your "trust" muscles to take advantage of opportunities. Find ways to minimize risks within these trust relationships. For example, configure project or venture so that breach of trust brings big negative consequences. If a person is looking to grow his or her business within a certain network or market in which you have a lot of influence, shape agreement so the individual understands the power your relationship brings and the loss he or she would experience if things didn't work out.

If you cannot establish a level of trust that will work for the project or venture, think about walking away for the time being. Often, people who enter agreements in these instances look for problems and micromanage others, which puts undue stress on the relationship and adds intangible and tangible costs to the project.

When considering entering, the current state of, or future of a trust relationship, ask yourself the following questions:

- How well will (or do) you demonstrate trustworthy behaviors?
- How well will (or does) the other person demonstrate trustworthy behaviors in this situation?
- What is the state of the relationship? Is it new, developing, or long sustained? Is it healthy or dysfunctional?
- Do you implicitly trust the person? With what things do you trust the person? With what things do you not trust the person?
- What do you like about the person and what can you rely on from that person?
- Is there any behavior that has to be confronted? If so, how are you going to handle it?
- What impact will trusting or not trusting a person have on the project or venture?
- What things can you do to build trust fast and strong?
- Are you focusing on costs or value creation? Conversations about value creation enable trust.
- What remedies do you have if things go wrong?

There are also different scenarios, e.g., new versus long-standing relationships, for applying trust in projects or ventures. Here are a few practical tips for projects around trust:

- Differentiate between projects that require working with people who need to earn your trust (on critical components) and those working with people who have already earned your trust.
- For projects/ventures working with people earning your trust, establish a manageable scope for six months to one year so that you can explore opportunities and relationships.
- Place critical components of a trust value chain, or a project, only in hands of people you implicitly trust.
- Develop a trust value chain from a core group of three to 12 people (a group that will hold each other accountable).
- Each group member, identify three people in business or professions they implicitly trust that fit the project/venture.
- Scope project/venture based on capacity within trust boundaries (for critical components).

You also need to assess the health of each key individual trust relationship periodically. In doing so, you need to decide if it needs maintaining, pruning, or cutting and take appropriate action.

Considerations for Value Network versus Trust Network

Focusing on individual trust relationships helps you discover the quality of the relationships within your network, which will help leverage available assets and resources. However, it's important to understand exactly what exchanges, flows, and deliverables occur within your network so you know what you can leverage.

While not covered here, it is easy enough to frame your network in terms of value by asking the following questions:

- Who are the people (or roles) in the network?
- What deliverables, exchanges, and flows occur in the network?
- Who is involved with each deliverable, exchange, and flow in the network?

- How well do the deliverables, exchanges, and flows occur with the people involved?
- From the previous elements, what value lies in the network?
- How can you improve and leverage the value in the network?

The best of all worlds is where you have a network filled with high-trust and high-value. Choices of whom to work with should be a combination of trust and the value each person brings. However, this is not a typical scenario unless you have been working on it with intent.

If you have a situation where someone brings high-value, but adequate trust is not present, see if you can discover a scope that allows for adequate trust and still takes advantage of the high-value the person brings. If you trust the person, but they do not bring sufficient value to the project, see if you can discover a scope that will bring forth the value and take advantage of the trust.

In either situation, if you cannot find an equation that brings both sufficient trust and value, I recommend that you walk away for the time being.

People and the Trust Network

This piece focused on how to leverage trust to transform global business opportunities. As with any methodology though, it can become mechanistic when focus is placed on the tasks and activities of managing trust rather than the people involved.

What was presented here should be used as a guideline and framework for facilitating trust relationships so you can see improved business performance. However, if you lose your connection to the people in the process, you defeat your initial purpose and the power of the trust network.

To keep yourself grounded, ask yourself the following questions:

- Do I care about the relationships and people within the network?
- Am I serving and looking out for the interests of the people in the network, even if it means sacrifices on my part?
- Is what I'm doing helping or harming people?
- What will I lose if I lose the trust of these people?
- Is what I am doing worth losing the trust?

Remember, the common denominator in any organization, community, society, market, or industry is the people involved. People are the reason that these spheres exist and people are the reason we are able to create wealth. If we harm or abuse them, it can at some point impact profitability.

Conclusion

Most consider trust an intangible asset, if an asset at all. But while it may not take physical form as currency, it is tangible in the behaviors exhibited by people in relationships.

High-trust relationships provide many benefits for businesses, including faster execution, lower costs, and even improved competitive advantage. These relationships situated in networks of business interests direct where flows of capital, information, resources, and assets go.

Trust networks employ the methodology of using trust, along with value, to configure business strategy for global business. Trust networks are developed in steps – from trust relationships, to trust value chains, to trust networks.

Individuals are the lowest common denominator in trust networks, so how individuals trust themselves and others and how well those relationships develop mutual trust, impact the health of the entire network.

Using a trust network to strategically leverage business opportunities is the macro level, but the trust network itself must be facilitated first and primarily through the micro level which are the relationships themselves.

16

Closing:
Challenges and Navigating the Path
Nissi Ekpott
Hartmut Sieper
Lauri Elliott

Even with all the positive paradigms shared about Africa in this book, there are still realities that need to be faced in Africa and ways to navigate your starting path that need to be shared. In this closing, we cover both.

Challenges
Africa presents one of the world's last big opportunities and in this book we have offered pointers towards these opportunities. However, doing business in Africa is not a bed of roses; on the contrary, investors need to be prepared for the challenges they may face.

Just like the European pioneers, who explored North America, faced and overcame its overwhelming challenges, those wanting to do business in Africa, at this phase of its development, need to see themselves as explorers, adventurers, and advancers in a new and fast emerging frontier. There are many challenges, and it would be impossible to discuss them all in this book, but here are a few to look out for.

Governance
Governance is improving. However, it is still far from ideal in many parts of the continent.

Conflict and Strife

From a peak of over 15 active wars in 1999, wars on the continent have reduced to less than five. However, there are still fragile areas within post-conflict nations, border areas, etc. There are pockets of local conflicts still happening.

It is necessary to carry out proper research about these areas, and avoid them, if possible. If working or doing business there is an absolute necessity, then seek practical advice on how to navigate and to reduce risk.

Security

Africa can be a dangerous place depending on where you are. Most countries are still in a recovery state, and though security is slowly improving, investors and visitors to the continent still need to approach these countries with care. Nigeria, Liberia, Sierra Leon,e and Kenya are showing improvements in their state of security. Rwanda has shown very rapid improvement and its capital, Kigali, is arguably one of Africa's safest cities.

Visiting and living in some parts of Africa may require that you change your lifestyle to adapt to local conditions. For instance, you may not be able to take walks on the streets, you may have to live behind high walls, and you may need security guards at entrance gates.

But not to worry, there are very practical ways to adapt. There are secure parks where you can walk, bike, walk your dog, or relax. In some places, such as South Africa, there are gated communities where you can find as much activity as you would require anywhere else. It is necessary for visitors to Africa to seek counsel and reside in safer areas.

Can't Trust Everyone

We've talked a lot about trust. However, it shouldn't be done blindly. Make wise choices.

If you are doing business in Africa, like everywhere else globally, do not trust people blindly. There are people who are simply out there to defraud. Do not take on a local business partner in a trusting and naive way. Make efforts to verify the credibility of the people you work with.

Can't Believe Everything You Hear

Do not believe all you hear especially from governments and state-run media, which is very rampant in Africa. Always try to hear the other side of the story from the ordinary people. Do sufficient independent research and then make informed decisions.

Bureaucracy

Africa is far more bureaucratic than your wildest imaginations. Licenses and registrations are needed for almost everything and it sometimes takes very long to achieve them. Some of these delays are just pure inefficiency, while others are deliberate opportunities for corruption.

Some African nations, such as Rwanda and Ghana, have been among global top reformers in improving their business processes, while others remain far behind. You need to find ways to absorb these delays into your overall project plan.

There are usually local agencies, such as business consultants, finance houses, and legal firms, who offer services to help foreign nationals process the myriad of local requirements. Sometimes it is advisable to use their services. They may seem expensive, but you will find out that they save you lots of time and actually work out cheaper in the long run than if you tried to do it yourself.

Corruption

Corruption remains a major challenge in most of Africa. The corruption is sometimes systemic and is not always recognized for what it is. But, bear in mind that there are many Africans who do not buy into corruption, and there will always be a way to navigate and avoid it.

UAC, a Nigerian company set up by the British over a hundred years ago, publicly declares that in its years of doing business in Nigeria it has never paid a bribe. Steve Shelley, author of *Doing Business in Africa*[86], a

---

[86] Shelley, S. (2004). *Doing Business in Africa: A Practical Guide for Investors, Entrepreneurs and Expatriate Managers.* New York, NY: Zebra Books.

British indigene who has lived and done business in at least twenty African countries over the past 25 years, states in his book that he has never had to be involved in corrupt practices.

Culture

An African country is not your country; there will be many differences in language, culture, and so on. Even if you speak the same language as the country you visit and in which you do business, look out for the fact that the meanings may be different.

Most African English-speaking countries, for instance, South Africa, Nigeria, and Kenya, have their own variety of English, and there are sometimes distinct differences. Cultures also differ from country to country, and in many cases some countries have differing cultures within them.

Nigeria, for instance, has over three hundred different ethnic groups, some with very distinct differences. Tanzania has over a hundred different ethnic groups, while South Africa has at least eleven.

In my (Nissi's) discussions with people who have visited Africa and decided to stay and do business, the one area that seems to be the biggest challenge has been cultural differences. Culture can make or break everything.

You need to be prepared for the differences in culture. Bear in mind that living in a place is different from visiting for a couple of weeks or months. This applies globally and Africa is no different.

Western visitors to South Africa are first amazed at the similarities to their nations in terms of look and feel, and then are shocked at the differences in terms of people and culture. Some things will be familiar to you, but many things different, and within individual countries there are many cultural differences. Some key cultural issues to watch out for:

- **Punctuality and time:** In most African cultures, time is like a flowing river, it is not exact, and there is no pressure to catch it because you can always get another part of it. Time based appointments are not expected to be kept. It sometimes applies differently to social functions than to official functions. In parts of

West Africa, it is actually against the norm to arrive for a wedding on time, and more acceptable to be there two hours late. For official meetings, it varies and generally, thirty minutes to one hour late may be acceptable. In dealing with government officials, you will find in some places that they may not turn up for the entire day, regardless of the appointments in their schedule. The increased usage of mobile phones has served to help; you can find out where the person you are meeting is, and decide if the scheduled time is realistic. Always try to get their phone numbers and call ahead, and always have another potential activity you could do with your time if a meeting is rescheduled or canceled. On the other hand, there are countries like Botswana where it is considered impolite when you come five minutes late.

- **Slow down:** Things do not move as fast in Africa.
- **Taking calls during meetings:** In some parts of Africa, such as South Africa, this is considered rude and generally not accepted except with the permission of the other people. However, in other countries, such as Nigeria, taking calls during meetings is acceptable.
- **Courtesy and social manners:** This occupies a place of high importance in most African cultures. Social greetings and exchanges are required, and you could lose a lot of respect for ignoring this. Handshakes, hugs, greetings, and small talk about the spouse and the family are part of the culture. These usually precede most conversations, including business.
- **Family:** African societies place high importance on family. People work from the basis of family. Because most African countries have an inefficient citizen tracking system, people rely on family relationships to establish credibility. Families are also very useful for arbitration and conflict resolution. There is usually a thin line between working through family networks and nepotism, but if you have to succeed in Africa, you need to come to terms that the culture works this way. People relate with each other beyond the individuals and reach out to their families.

- **Dress code:** In most parts of Sub-Saharan Africa, formal dressing is required for formal occasions, such as business meetings, church events, and so on. This is regardless of the hot climate. Some parts are sensitive to women's and men's clothing. Women visiting Africa should take care to ask about the dress codes.

- **Entertaining and social events:** Most African cultures are very much into entertaining and social functions, everything calls for a celebration – a marriage, birthday, burial, and festive seasons - and it is usually a large celebration. Huge crowds turn up for seemingly unimportant events. And you will be expected to attend. So, sharpen your social skills!

- **Language:** Most people in Africa speak at least two languages – one of the main languages, i.e., English or French, and a local language. These main languages are usually the common language within a nation and help them overcome the wide ethnic and language diversity. However, keep in mind that it is usually not their first language and hence may be expressed in a way different to what you understand. Always try to clarify things, and keep discussions simple.

- **Business expenses:** These can be very high in many parts of Africa. Sometimes where there is no consistent electricity, you need to factor in the cost of a backup generator and the fuel to run it. In some cities, such as Lagos, you may find it easier to get yourself a chauffeur. This is an added cost. Salaries are low, but sometimes this advantage is stolen by low productivity. Investors should place a premium on employee training and improving work ethics and productivity. Manufactured items are mostly imported, so they are more expensive in many parts of the continent, these include things like vehicles, electronic equipment, phones, etc.

- **Diseases:** Malaria, HIV/AIDS, and several other diseases are rampant in Africa. The high prevalence of these diseases affects worker productivity, and in many parts of the continent, citizens do not have health insurance services, so investors need to factor this in while planning. Foreign visitors should ensure they have necessary vaccinations.

- **Poor infrastructure especially in West and Central Africa:** The roads can be very bad and in many cases non-existent. As much as possible, travel should be done by air. Where road travel is unavoidable, make provision for the delays. Where you can, avoid on-land, cross border travel as these places can be quite corrupt at times. Electricity supply can be epileptic in some parts, so if you have to set up private residence, you need to think of standby power. Since the water infrastructure is poor in some places and non-existent in others, you may need to consider buying bottled water, or drilling a borehole.

These are just a summary of things to look at. In the book, *Doing Business in Africa* by Steve Shelley, you will find a lot more detail on the day-to-day issues you may face, and recommendations on how to tackle these. Remember, Africa consists of 53 countries (soon to be 54 countries with the addition of Southern Sudan), and these challenges are not necessarily found in all the countries. Some parts of Africa can favorably match western standards in varying ways.

Navigating the Path

We have shared some of the many opportunities available in Africa with a few core approaches to consider for doing business in the New Africa. However, it is astounding the number of opportunities that lie fallow. I think of the example I was told by a Mozambican professional who said every season scores of mangos just rot on the road side because there are no processing facilities to make juice, frozen, or canned products.

So, how do you get started with tapping into the opportunities in Africa? We have pointed out the methodology for shaping your business strategy around opportunities presented through your trust networks. This is the anchor, but there is a process to carry out which is the focus of this section.

First, I (Lauri) want to mention that not everyone will want to venture into business themselves, but will be willing to invest. In fact, investing is often a preferred method for people since they do not need to become an expert but can rely on those who are to create successful ventures and partnering with them to do so.

If you are into stocks, you can look at how to diversify your portfolio to include firms that operate in Africa. There are several mechanisms for tapping publicly listed companies on over 20 stock exchanges in Africa as shared here.

You can also invest in private ventures directly or indirectly. There are venture projects for which people are looking for investors. At another level, you can invest in a private equity fund, which is managed by a fund manager and consists of several or many projects. You can contact Hartmut (www.trans-africa-invest.com) to learn more.

Some of you have ideas for products and services that you want to export to the African markets or import from African markets to the U.S. and other global regions. Nissi (www.neuafrika.com) has terrific insights into the African markets and can assist with importing and exporting products, as well as establishing a business there.

One key recommendation beyond working with people that you trust is that whether you invest or decide to do business in Africa, don't go it alone. If you are going to invest, think about forming an investment club with several people to share the experience and spread the risk. If you are going to form a business, find strategic business partners on your side of the world not just local partners in Africa. While it can sometimes be challenging to work with a group, your collective learning, insights, and perspectives can create substantial intangible assets as you develop more projects.

Emerging Market Strategy Framework

More than anything else that will affect us today in business is the fluid, dynamic, and complex nature of interactions. Strategy can no longer be a straight, strict, logical path. Strategy must incorporate moving dynamics and complexity.

In our work, we call this process weaving, or shaping, strategy. Central to the rationale for this approach is that people sit at the center of every business and interaction. Therefore, it is important to understand the relationships and flows (capital, information, resources, etc.) around them. Thus, our approach is within the context of networks instead of formal structures although the people within these structures are a part of the networks and the formal structures also help define boundaries, as well as serve as centers of authority, resources, capital, and information.

Our framework is called the *7x7 Emerging Market Strategy Framework* – seven components and seven steps. The components, or lenses, of this framework include business concepts, trust networks, value creation, optimization (minimizing negative variables like risk and maximizing impact), leverage points, business and investment strategies, and market definition, access, and flow. These components are woven together through a seven-step process:

1. Identification and classification of assets
2. Assessment and structuring of trust and value networks
3. Clarification of context, both current and future, in the emerging market (e.g., Africa)
4. Identification and creation of feasible business concepts and scenarios
5. Development and prioritization of strategic options
6. Optimization of prioritized business concepts and ventures (reducing cost, mitigating risk, maximizing impact)
7. Implementation and ongoing evaluation

This approach works well for large, medium, and small ventures. However, the next section outlines a more streamlined approach for maximizing opportunities through developing small, significant, and scalable greenfield projects or start-up ventures.

Navigating Small, but Significant Opportunities

Many of you will be starting ventures on a small scale with limited resources. In the case of my firm, Conceptualee, we have dozens of small-scale projects with a lot of potential. So, we have to maximize our resources so we can develop many greenfield projects and start-up ventures simultaneously.

This early stage development is normally a killer for most ventures because people and organizations sink too many resources and capital upfront while creating debt before generating cash flow. We, on the other hand, bootstrap all of our projects and ventures, particularly until they reach a stage they can be commercialized and we can expect ongoing revenue. There will be exceptions at times, however.

We also focus on the principles of using our strengths, using what we have in hand, and tapping into other resources through our networks. Our goal is to allow us to flow with the market opportunities that fit our strengths. In doing so, we find a lot of "hidden" gems. We live by the Leverage Point Strategy™.

While there are many aspects to consider when starting a greenfield project or start-up venture, there is a process and basic set of tools that you can use to shape these opportunities. I have developed a methodology called Going Global on a Dime™[87], which is particularly suited to start-up and emerging market environments.

Start-up ventures and greenfield projects typically have a life of three to five years before they transform into more formal entities or die. The Going Global on a Dime™ methodology focuses on the first stage of this period – both the conceptualization and initial implementation.

The first six months focus on identifying, shaping, planning, and launching the business venture. The following steps are generally completed in this order, but can be iterative in nature:

1. Identify your strengths, or capital assets, which may be both tangible and intangible.
2. Conduct initial research to learn more about opportunities, sources, countries, markets, and global issues that will help shape your strategy. Research is a continual process throughout this three- to six-month period.
3. Learn about issues that impact your business globally and in a particular country, e.g., regulations, labor laws, countries and

---

[87] http://www.goingglobalonadime.com

products which are banned by your government, intellectual property.

4. Develop your company and product brand. Once you define your brand, you also need to produce a profile, brochure, website, business cards, and other appropriate marketing materials.

5. Go out (both online and offline) to explore your networks to identify people and organizations with which you can potentially work. Build your ecosystem to support the value chain you will have to develop to carry out the venture.

6. Prioritize opportunities based on your strengths, including your ecosystem. Continue with high priority opportunities.

7. Draft an initial business model for each of the high priority opportunities. You only want to work on 1-3 opportunities at a time.

8. Use the business models as discussion documents to draw partners and resources. Resist the urge to approach investors until you have a concrete plan.

9. After your discussions and after you have chosen the one opportunity to pursue, flush out customer profile, as well as supply chain and marketing channels to customer.

10. Flush out revenue and operational model, as well as cost structure.

11. Develop a concept document, which will be used to frame your business venture.

12. Sign non-disclosure/non-compete agreements with partners, investors, providers, etc.

13. Develop initial project plan, budget, and cash flow projections for the first year of the venture.

14. Shape your business strategy to work within the scope and parameters that will leverage your assets, keep costs low, have potentially significant outcomes that can be scaled, and will accelerate cash flow.

15. Sign joint venture agreement (based on outlined business strategy) and finalize project plan and budget.
16. Implement and operate first-year plan.[88]
17. Monitor progress and adapt as necessary.
18. Conduct quarterly reviews of business.
19. Conduct a review of the first year.
20. Determine next phase of business operation.

During this initial stage, it is important to leverage assets that you have and minimize risk, some pointers include:

- Look for low-hanging fruit and opportunities.
- Do sufficient due diligence as befits the size of investment.
- Choose small, but significant opportunities that can be scaled.
- Resist the urge to go into debt in early-stage ventures.
- Include people that you have strong trust relationships as part of your core team.
- Don't promise or expect too much from partners.
- Be honest and open to promote transparency, but be wise in what, how, to whom, and when you share.
- Conduct regular status meetings and prepare reports. (Some Africans do not prefer to write, so you can do an oral report and take good notes.)
- Expect change and be willing to adapt.

Conclusion

You will find investing in Africa a profitable learning curve. You will encounter a spirit of enterprise like you have never experienced, all across the continent. You will see unbridled hope, optimism, laughter, celebration, and zeal in the midst of many challenges. Investing, living, or working among Africans will change your life, not only financially, but in every other way, too.

---

[88] For a sample plan, send an email to info@conceptualee.com.

Not all that looks good is actually good, and not all that looks bad, is really bad. Sometimes great gifts come in ugly packages.

The story is told that the first diamonds to be discovered in Kimberly, South Africa, were found by kids who thought it was just a bright stone and kicked it around and played with it. The diamond eventually found its way into the right hands, and the rest is history – the economy of that nation changed forever. A lot of Africa is like a diamond in the rough.

Also, you will never find the perfect time for venturing out into Africa, so it's important to have the frame of mind to be committed to doing it. Any path of promise has its giants, so expect challenges but also expect success.

And finally, Africa is a "big" place with so much to offer. It's like getting a big dose of oxygen into your system. So, as you experience it and its people, let your spirit be enlivened.

Appendix A:
African New Economy Workgroup (ANEW)

Hartmut, Nissi, and Lauri are the lead facilitators for the African New Economy Workgroup (ANEW). The purpose of ANEW is to catalyze and accelerate economic opportunity and development in Africa and the diaspora that is open, inclusive, and benefits all by approaching our social/informal/business networks and global value chains as a single economy.

ANEW is an open organism welcoming all who can "connect" with its vision and abide by its ethical framework to release the tapped wealth in Africa to its people and through its people bring wealth to the world.

How Does ANEW Describe an Economy?

An economy is a system of production, exchange, distribution, and consumption of goods and services. It is a system of creating, increasing, and transforming value.

However, ANEW sees an economy as both a platform for exchange and community. In fact, ANEW's economy is constructed based on people and their relationships. It takes a human ecological view of economy in which people are the foci and all other elements support the prosperity of people. Therefore, institutions, processes, procedures, etc., serve people not the other way around.

In essence, ANEW's economy is a social network transformed to a value network – a network that has a purpose. In this case, the purpose is to promote economic prosperity along the African trade routes. The economy is held together by the trust that exists between the people in ANEW.

The economic system assures that economic justice, opportunity, and prosperity is spread to active "citizens" of ANEW.

The economy takes on a unique configuration of elements from virtual, geographic, and alternative economies. Its scope is expansive, but aligns with its objectives. It is not defined by a rigid framework.

The nature of the economy is self-sustaining, growing/expanding, and able to handle the turbulent, fast, and chaotic environment of today. It does this by maintaining an organic, fluid state, which is achieved by agility.

The ANEW economy will be a model for what we call a "conduit" economy.

What is ANEW's Key Message?

Exploring, embracing, engaging, and expanding to alternative markets in and through Africa to create exponential opportunities for growing sustainable business and fostering and maximizing benefits to all key stakeholders.

The future of our world is multi-polar, meaning that one or a few countries will no longer hold the economic or political power over the entire world. Instead, each country will have its own unique space and strengths in all spheres, including economic, political, and cultural. Our world will move fluidly and dynamically, where possible, like living systems interconnected.

In terms of the global economy, this means creating multi-growth poles - stimulating and catalyzing growth in every region and leveraging for global growth instead of relying on growth in one or a few countries like the United States in the past to fuel growth. There will, of course, be countries that will represent larger growth opportunities at different stages based on different variables like size of population. Good examples are China and India.

Every perspective, or every growth region, will provide opportunities in their local, regional, and global markets. This holds true for Africa and Africa is already positioned to serve as one pole, an epicenter, and an open gateway to trade, investment, and business to emerging markets like Brazil, China, India, and Russia, and even to the developed world.

The key phrase in our message is "alternative" markets. What we mean by "alternative" markets are markets in addition to your existing market not necessarily instead of. This approach is based on the principle of alternative, multiple, or diversified streams of revenue. If we think of economies, more diversified economies typically can withstand external shocks better and this is what you want to do for your enterprise so you can continue to grow and generate profit.

When we speak of markets, it could refer to places like Nigeria, China, Vietnam, and Argentina. But markets also mean different things, e.g., industries, online, microniches, and metamarkets. When you think about the word "market," think outside of the normal definition for markets. This will help you see more opportunities.

When we talk about opportunities, there is a simple principle called adjacent opportunities. Adjacent opportunities, coined by Ronald Schultz, are those that are only a step away and came into existence because of previous actions. So, if you never go through the process of exploring, embracing, engaging, and expanding in and through Africa, you will not likely discover nor apprehend the exponential opportunities for growing sustainable businesses available by connecting with Africa.

When you explore, it means taking a look at potential opportunities by doing initial research, talking with people, etc. When you embrace, it means deciding that you will pursue Africa as a channel to create exponential growth opportunities for your business. When you engage, it means acting on that decision. And, when you expand, it means finally implementing one, several, or many of the opportunities. These activities are part of an iterative process called E^4.

And finally, notice that we say "in and through" Africa. Africa is not only positioned to be a pole of growth in itself, but as a conduit for global business and trade. Africa has become an epicenter and open gateway for international trade. This has quietly snuck up on the world.

What is ANEW Doing Now?

2011 is the year in which ANEW will initiate its "conduit" economy with specific projects. These projects include gold mining, agriculture, ICT, media and broadcasting, and importing and exporting channels. The projects will be in and through Africa and to emerging markets like Brazil, India, and China, as well as to the United States, Germany, and other developed countries. For more information, send an email to anew@conceptualee.com.

Lauri Elliott

Lauri's primary role and gifting is as a strategist. She has over 25 years of business experience, specializing in global business, innovation, technology, and new ventures and start-ups. She serves entrepreneurs, small, micro, and medium-size enterprises (SMMEs), and individual investors.

As the Director of Afribiz™ Media, a Division of Conceptualee, Inc., Lauri has developed a solid reputation as a new media leader. She is the primary host of Afribiz.fm™, a regular online radio show about doing business and investing in Africa. She also writes frequently for publications such as *Brainstorm* magazine, an ITWeb publication, in South Africa.

In addition, Lauri is the author of *Export to Explode Cash Flow and Profits: Creating New Streams of Business in Asia, Africa, and the Americas* and *Going Global on a Dime: The Entrepreneur's Handbook to Tapping the Global Marketplace*.

Lauri sits on the board of advisers for the Center for Global Entrepreneurship and Enterprise Management (CGEEM) at Morgan State University, which focuses on equipping U.S. SMEs to enter international business. In this capacity, she is leading the development of the Emerging Market Information Team (EMIT), designed to provide information and intelligence particularly useful to SMEs. For her work on behalf of SMEs, she received recognition from the U.S. Congress for connecting U.S. businesses to business in Africa.

In addition to encouraging SMEs in the U.S., Lauri is also committed to the development of SMEs in emerging markets. While in South Africa from 2005 to 2008, she fostered local economic development systems driven by youth enterprises.

To reach Lauri, visit http://www.lauri-elliott.com.

Hartmut Sieper

Hartmut is a banker, business consultant, and investment specialist. Hartmut is convinced that the time has come for Africa to arise in many aspects, including business and finance. In anticipating this trend, he has founded the company Trans Africa Invest to attract businesses, companies, and investors from German-speaking countries to African markets. He is working closely together with local partners in 15 African countries. He is the sole investment adviser of a Luxembourg-based, Pan-African mutual fund which is investing in listed African securities.

He has written several books about investing. His latest books are *Investing in Africa - The Wealth of the Black Continent* and *Cape of Good Business - Strategies for Long-Term Success in South Africa* (both are written in German), as well as *Tapping the Wealth of African Stocks*. In the German media, he is considered as one of the leading Africa experts in Germany.

Hartmut is married and lives in northern Bavaria, Germany. Hartmut can be reached at http://www.trans-africa-invest.com.

Nissi Ekpott

Nissi is an entrepreneur, business developer, and catalyst for African restoration. Raised in Nigeria, he started his first business – a dry cleaning service - at the age of 15. Over the years, he gained experience through conventional education, and several hands-on experiences.

Nissi consults for small and big businesses in Africa, touching business and leadership development and providing services, including business tours and training programs for public and private sector officials.

Nissi coordinates BizConnect Afrika, a place businesses connect, as well as share ideas, opportunities, and resources. He also serves as a business journalist for Afribiz.net, a media brand of Conceptualee, Inc. (U.S.) and other websites and magazines in South Africa.

He lives in Johannesburg, South Africa with his wife and two beautiful daughters. To reach Nissi, visit http://www.neuafrika.com.

Other Contributors

Nwakego Eyisi

http://www.nwakegoeyisi.com

Nwakego Linda Eyisi is co-founder of Encompass Analytic of Nigeria, a research and business intelligence firm serving clients like MTN of Nigeria. She is a trained and experienced economist, who specialized in the pharmaceutical industry for many years.

Nwakego serves as a featured Afribiz columnist and occasional radio host for Afribiz.fm. She covers key economic forums for Afribiz, including G20, African Union, regional economic community, and trade bloc events.

Jonathan Goldberg

http://www.globalbusiness.co.za

In his quest for knowledge, Jonathan has accumulated a B.Comm degree (Bachelor in Commerce), a LL.B (Baccalaureus Legum) degree, a Honours in Business Administration (HBA) degree (cum laude), a Masters in Business Administration (MBA) degree (cum laude). Jonathan founded Global Business Solutions (where he still holds the position of CEO), which has become a leading business consultancy focusing on strategic interventions, including training, labor law, and business-to-business solutions in the area of broad-based black economic empowerment.

Johnny co-authored *Cracking Broad-Based Black Economic Empowerment* in 2005 (the first published authority in South Africa) and *Broad-Based Black Economic Empowerment: Final Codes and Scorecard* in 2008 (a complete rework to the first publication). Over and above consulting to a range of enterprises on black economic empowerment, Jonathan has facilitated various high profile BBBEE business transactions.

John Luiz

http://wits.academia.edu/JohnLuiz

John Luiz is a Professor at the Wits Business School (University of the Witwatersrand), South Africa, specializing in International Business Strategy, Business, Society, and Government, and the Economics of Emerging Markets. He also serves as their Director of International Programmes and formerly as Academic Director. Previously, he was Executive Dean in the Faculty of Management at the University of Johannesburg.

Besides winning various teaching awards, John has published in excess of 50 articles in leading journals including: Applied Economics, World Development, Oxford Economic Papers, Journal of Development Studies, The International Review of Law and Economics, etc. He is the co-author and/or editor of several books published by Macmillan, Pearson and Oxford University Press, including *Managing Business in Africa: Practical Management Theory for an Emerging Market.*

John works as a consultant and has undertaken research for the African Development Bank in Tunisia, Development Bank of Southern Africa, the Industrial Development Corporation, the Department of Trade and Industry, the United States Agency for International Development, the Johannesburg Development Agency, and the Centre for Development and Enterprise, among others.

BizConnect Afrika

www.bizconnectafrika.biz

*You want to get into Africa and do business,
but you do not know anyone in Africa.*

- How do you find credible networks and connect to real business people?
- How do you find "on the ground" information?
- How do you test your ideas and share ideas and resources?
- How do you gain a relational entry point into the continent?

BizConnect Afrika is a business network established to share ideas, opportunities, and resources between its members. BizConnect Afrika is designed to encourage the building of relationships and community through business. It is a virtual/face-to-face business network that bridges and connects businesses beyond borders.

BizConnect Afrika members realize that even though business is good, business deals are temporal while relationships are eternal. Hence, relationship and community building is necessary for true success.

Visit the BizConnect Afrika website at *www.bizconnectafrika.biz*. Register online and become part of a business community with a focus on Africa.

Trans Africa Invest

www.trans-africa-invest.com

You want to invest in Africa, but you do not know how.

- How do you find investment projects in specific sectors and countries where you can invest?
- How do you find reliable investment managers with strong local expertise in Africa, who are following business practices that are described in this book?
- How do you reduce investment risk?

Trans Africa Invest is a Germany-based investment and consultancy firm that introduces investors, companies, and technologies from developed countries into African growth markets.

Through private equity (PE) funds, which are launching in 2011, investors can choose viable projects in various African countries and different economic sectors in which to invest. An international team of investment professionals, both from Africa and the developed world, will manage the PE funds and support the portfolio companies in doing their businesses, thereby adding value to the portfolios. The PE funds will be domiciled in a well-known financial center, i.e. Mauritius. In 2011, we are specifically looking for:

- Viable projects in Africa (business plan is required)
- Investors that want to have exposure in Africa in a broad range of attractive projects in various countries
- Financial intermediaries in U.S. and selected European countries that will connect domestic investors with African investment projects, either by participating in our private equity funds or by creating joint ventures

Afribiz

www.afribiz.info

You want to learn more about business in Africa,
but you don't know where to go.

Afribiz.info is the leading, and premier, independent portal about doing
business and investing in Africa.

Afribiz provides free and premium resources, intelligence, information, tools, insights, and strategies to help you navigate business and investment in Africa. If you want to know something about business in Africa, Afribiz is the best place to start.

Afribiz.info is our portal bringing together resources about African business from around the world into one place. No need to find resources one by one. We help you accelerate your research and strategy efforts.

Afribiz.net is the site for our premium, mostly original content provided as text, audio, and video that can be interacted with across computing and mobile platforms.

Afribiz.fm (www.blogtalkradio.com/afribiz) is our publicly broadcast audio content. Hear from experts and entrepreneurs how they make things happen in business in Africa. This is no ordinary program. You hear and learn what you can do to make things happen for you.

We also develop publications, e.g., books, magazines, and guides, conduct webinars and teleconferences (live and on-demand), host face-to-face events, and provide facilitation and consulting to help you navigate business in Africa successfully.

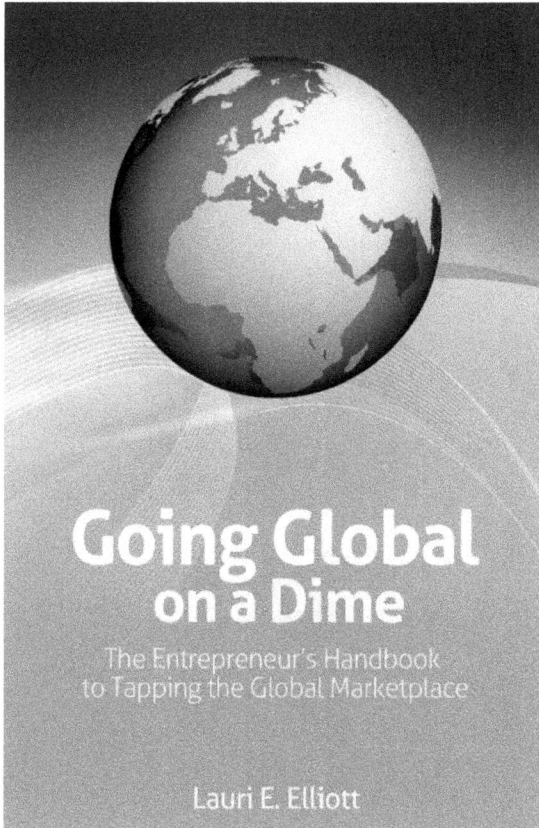

www.goingglobalonadime.com

Going Global on a Dime answers the "how" of going global from both a strategic and practical approach, focusing on new and existing firms considering or just starting the going global process. It re-wires the framework for going global so firms can navigate the course dynamically while minimizing costs, managing and maximizing cash flow and return on investment, streamlining processes, and keeping the "small" firm ready to take advantage of profitable opportunities.

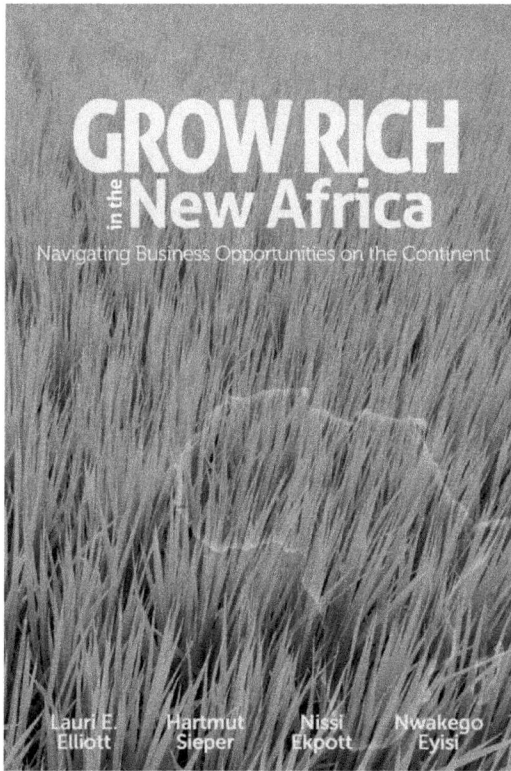

www.grow-rich-in-the-new-africa.com

Grow Rich in the New Africa attempts to present a number of opportunities and strategies so that entrepreneurs, investors, and SMEs can piece together unique strategy configurations to be successful in Africa. It extends the coverage first presented in *Redefining Business in the New Africa*. Some of what you will learn includes:

- Global trends and Africa
- Networks of players in Africa
- Business, trade, resource, and information flows in and out of Africa
- The future of major sectors, e.g., energy, real estate, transport, natural resources, retail markets
- Building strategy around both formal and informal markets

INVESTING

Tapping the Wealth of African Stocks

Building a Valuable Stock Portfolio

Hartmut Sieper

www.tapping-wealth-of-african-stocks.com

Warren Buffet says, "The critical investment factor is determining the intrinsic value of a business and paying a fair or bargain price." Where can investors go to find these businesses today?

Africa is one place. "African stocks continue to be undervalued, providing greater value for investors interested in long-term investments," says Hartmut Sieper, the author. *Tapping the Wealth of African Stocks* focuses on helping individual investors understand how to access African stock markets.

www.export-to-explode-cash-flow.com

Exporting is one of the strategies for conducting international business or trade. With the *squeeze* on businesses during the global economic recovery, there is no better time to explore new avenues to generate revenues and profits. *Export to Explode Cash Flow and Profits* specifically shares 12 different leverage points, e.g., demand-driven exporting, multinational ecosystems, and cities and economic hubs that you can use to help formulate strategies for exporting to the emerging markets in Asia, Africa, and the Americas.